Just
Roll Over
And
Float

For Lizzie,
Great Blessing
of joyful laughter.
Lesley Michaels

Lesley Michaels

Be Life Publications
P.O. Box 28028
Santa Fe, NM 87592

Just Roll Over and Float
by Lesley Michaels

ISBN 978-1-881099-87-1
First printing – February 2008
Second Printing – January 2012

Printed in the United States of America and New Zealand

0   1   2   3   4   5   6   7   8   9

For all the dear ones who traveled this path with me.

The vibration of our thoughts is a magnetic beacon—a signal sent into the vastness, which then captures what we believe and manifests it physically into our lives.

-Carol Ann Jerome

Table of Contents

Introduction

The Divine Feminine is a much talked about expression in these days of great confusion on our planet. There is conversation of Her coming back to us, of Her integrating into who we are, and of the movement to re-embrace Her as a living presence. But what exactly is this Divine Feminine? At the most basic level, it is half of who we each are. The Divine Feminine and the Divine Masculine are the primary elements of our souls; just as DNA is the foundation of our physical selves. In actuality, it is not just the time of the resurrection of the Divine Feminine, but of the Divine Masculine as well. In short, the two are who we are at our most core levels. They are the most authentic self that we have the potential to be, in each moment of our lives.

It is true that She has come back to active expression on and within the planet, and is now being followed by the Divine Masculine, but not from some distant place. The Divine Feminine and Masculine have been and are resurrecting themselves from the deepest recesses within our beings and within the planet's core. This great shimmering golden presence is rising out of exile and coming to the surface of our awareness to play once again. This is their goal, to play, to bring their Lightness of Being into our hearts and lives, as they remind us how to be the living presence of joy while also knowing the freedom of expressions available through our human experience.

This time of coming home—re-birthing—within our awareness is a reminder that we are not here to cling to ourselves or any aspect of our lives. It is time to set down our exaggerated attempts to reach and stretch for peace, for love, for inner comfort. Through these inner entanglements we have continued to hold ourselves in restriction. We have held the belief in some small hidden part of our mind, that after another has proven their love for us, we will finally feel safe to fully open our hearts and return that love. We have searched for peace, convincing ourselves that when it arrives, as if by magic, we will then—and only then—be able to take in that long awaited deep breath and relax into a state of ease.

Now our own Divine Presence is calling for us to awaken, and to play in our natural state of bliss, to unclench our fists and flow into the peace that is innate to our beings. Within this invitation, we are offered the opportunity to become rich with expressions of delight, to overflow with laughter, and to dare to love boldly and unabashedly, no longer confined by a perpetual fear of loss. In this new day, we will find ourselves ready to flow into complete awareness, that in every moment in which we open fully to these authentic expressions of who we are, we become more.

These self-expressions are rising into our minds and into our lives to remind us that we need not *seek* peace, joy, or wholeness, for that is who we are. Our natural state of completeness is reawakening within to remind us that we are infinitely wise, and to support us in celebrating the fullness of that as a living reality.

Our inner wisdom is speaking to us, whispering into our ears, "Remember the truth of who you are, remember the trust—of all that you are, of all that is." Trust is the essential component of love. And to be without one is to lack the other. As we re-embrace a full experience of self-trust, we discover the place of fully letting go. It is in these moments our deepest memory awakens to the certainty that we are the most precious friend we will ever have in this life. Trust is the springboard that guides us to never again betray ourselves.

As we embrace a renewed trust of our own beings, choices and movements, we find ourselves falling into a space of love that is deeper and more penetrating than what we have ever known or even dared to imagine. Through the doorway of trust, we are finally able to fall passionately in love, *with ourselves*.

One of the primary obstacles we have repeatedly encountered while stretching for the ability to relax and let go is our absence of understanding the subtle, yet significant difference between letting go and giving up. So many times we have just given up—out of exhaustion, out of confusion, or out of a lack of ability to determine any next step. This is not the same as letting go. The act of letting go is based in trusting something greater than the limited vision we have held of "self," and entrusting our lives to that greater personal expression. Letting go is making a choice, then moving forward with what you can do to generate its fulfillment while maintaining an openness to what has remained—until now—unexpected internal support and input.

Within each of us lives a calmer, more authentic self, which has been waiting patiently for us to release all vestiges of control, so that it can leap to our assistance. Now, practice exhaling and just letting go. This is the gateway to trust. Moving from an exhibition of self-trust, we invite that greater whole that we are—the expression of our own innate wisdom—to create an expansion within our lives that is beyond any we have considered possible. It is only through this embrace and continuation of trust that we are able to move into a broader acceptance of sincere happiness than we have ever envisioned.

The journey to peace and wholeness has proven to be a long and winding path, and arrival at that destination has seemed ever elusive. In truth, we don't actually want the end we have been seeking. An end would only offer stagnation, boredom, and an absence of any continuation of fulfillment.

In reality, there is no destination; simply acknowledge that this journey has no end. The pursuit of a specific, but indefinable destination has become one of the primary hindrances in the pursuit of personal freedom. The very conflict created by desiring an outcome that is both specific and indefinable instills great confusion within our minds. Destination is nothing more than an idea, an illusion created by the mind.

We are beings of great fluidity. As we breathe into our expanding presence, the creative pulse that fuels our endless capacity reaches into every expression of life. To limit the movement of that flexibility to a single idealized place or perspective is to restrict our unlimited potential. To release the fallacy of idealizing any mental vision as a specific and desirable destination, we must be ready—not just willing—but ready, to embrace all that we are, *just as we are.*

Many speak of the pursuit for peace, or a longing for joy. In truth, without realizing it, most people are simply seeking to be *less* miserable than what they have been. This is revealed through statements such as, "If I just had this" or "If I could just accomplish that."

Set down all limited visions of one single idea being the ultimate path to peace, and open your heart and senses to discover the whole of who you are. This action calls to the entirety of your natural inheritance to rise gently into the days and experiences of your life.

The deep penetrating *wanting* of peace is the greatest barrier standing between our current existence and the realization of it. Wanting spawns the idea of needing, which erupts into the belief that these states rest beyond one's current reach. Therefore, it is through longing, wanting, and stretching that the struggle is given sufficient oxygen to persist. The deeper the wanting, the greater the struggle. The greater the struggle, the more the dreaded misery is nurtured and fed. Through these cycles, one constantly distances themselves further and more restrictively from these seemingly mysterious elements of happiness.

Within the search for peace and joy rests the common belief that having attained them, there will be no more tears, no more sadness, no more journeys. However, the truth of our inner world is that we represent the fullest spectrum of beingness ever expressed.

Only through accepting our entire selves and all the emotions and sensory pulses that communicate themselves through us can we realize that the wholeness we have been seeking has always been alive—within. As we let go, exhale deeply, we set ourselves free to welcome and openly experience the happy moments and joyous times, as well as the unknowing and tearful occasions of life. We become truly alive. Ceasing to sanction only a portion of ourselves to include the completeness of our emotional, sensory spectrum is the ultimate act of self-acceptance, the doorway to self-trust.

Allowing flow to the already existent presence of peace and joy that rests within is an invitation to our own beings to demonstrate such self-trust as to own our experiences of sadness and to become unafraid to feel our own fears. To stop running from the less comfortable revelations offered by our emotional sensations, finally opens the door to full comprehension of the peace and joy, long sought.

Are you ready to play like a child, ready to feel foolish and silly, and still love yourself after? Are you ready to love and be loved in return, to be bold enough to make a mistake, or what you *judge* as a mistake, and not play in self condemnation? Are you ready to wake up and be life? If so, stop chasing what you envision as the destination and feel—in your body, in your cells, and through your experiences—what truly fills you. The key to these expressions of life is found by relaxing into full inner acceptance, which is the creative fiber of each of us. Are you ready to be all that you—already are?

These pages are a map. It is not traditional in its presentation, yet it is rich in its potential. This is a map of the joy available by being human, and in that, it is a map of you, from an all-encompassing understanding. The roads outlined are the pathways out of the fog of self-minimization and into the radiance of who you are in the fullness of your most authentic presentation. The mental conflict that has directed your life and the lives of each of us can now be eased into its own completion. The map offered here will guide you into a full understanding of this mental tug-o-war—what it is, how it responds to life, and how we became so very afraid of life itself.

Within the understanding of the many faces of mental conflict is the doorway to healing the unsettled mind and through that, its release from its own anguish. Simple understanding is the healing and therein your point of passage to blossoming into the full authentic playfulness that is your truth, your Light, and ultimately the source of all you could ever desire to experience.

Part I

Making Sense

The World of Physicality

There is a veritable wealth of religious and spiritual doctrines that detail how and why we became so disassociated from the peace, trust and joy of our innate natures. Each frames their story in accordance with their own finely tuned perspective.

Within many of these traditions we are now witnessing expanding conversation about the reemergence of the Divine Feminine, the Feminine Principle, the Feminine Expression, and any other number of terminologies.

Most simply, we have come to understand that where there is yin there is also yang. Therefore, what we are experiencing is a reawakening of our own inner Divine expressions of both feminine and masculine, yin and yang.

A most essential understanding within this reemergence is that our period of being "disassociated with" these levels of our innate wisdom was not synonymous to being "dismembered from." We did not fall from grace. Our Divine spark has not been taken from us, like bad little children being harshly punished. This amazing planet is not a place of exile or karmic penalty through which we must work and toil to prove a specific level of worthiness, all to earn our release into a more desirable level of existence.

Each of these varying and often conflicting stories of old has a single consistent thread. They are each a variation on the tale of having been reduced to human form as a punishment for having lost or abandoned our original expression of purity. The stories go on to chronicle how we were given human experience as a means of cleansing ourselves of all that was contaminated so we may again be worthy of greater heights. Then after—and only after—we have proven this beyond any measure of doubt will we rise to heaven, ascend to a higher realm, be released of the karmic wheel or experience emancipation from our exile through any number of other trajectories.

Over the multiple generations, what these stories and their projected expectations have effectively accomplished is to imbed within our sub-conscious minds, cellular and genetic memories the belief that we are untrustworthy, undeserving and sure to endure a long and arduous struggle in proving otherwise.

With the resurrection of our Divine awareness from the internally dormant space to which we have limited it, comes the reminder that we are each as much connected to our innate wisdom, inner joy and life-generating passion, as we have ever been. These are each parts of the natural spiral of our soul, our very beingness. The Divine Feminine and Divine Masculine are reawakening to support us in realizing that we have simply forgotten our presence as valued co-creators within this world.

Their internal revitalization will remind us that we did not come to this Earth to be reporters, or spectators of, the physical world. What sparked our enthusiasm was the promise of the opportunity to *engage in* the smorgasbord of enticing delights, available only while in physical body. By remaining fully open to our experiences of touch, taste, scent, hearing and sight we spontaneously begin to fully inhabit our physical selves. From here we gently settle back into the center of each moment in which we find ourselves. Everything in this universe, on this planet, within our individual beings that is true, sincere, authentic and filled with life can be experienced only from the point of *now*. Any time we distance from our senses we create internal separation. This positions us on the outskirts of our lives, peering in, rather than fully engaging.

It is only from the point of *now* that we can release all judgment to begin playing with new expressions of self-acceptance. This is what affords us reinvigoration of full-bodied self-trust. Through the rebirth of self-trust we naturally, organically, give ourselves permission to live from the center of every experience. One extraordinary gift we receive only when we rest in the center of the moment, life, ourselves, our experiences is an ever-flowing conscious connection with our own spark of both the Divine Feminine and Masculine.

How are we to hear and establish flowing communication with the inner voice of our more complete self? By resting into the moment of *now*, the center of all we are. The most accessible entrance to these center points is through our physical senses. With the prevailing story of our arrival in this world being for the pure purpose of earning our way back to something finer, it is only natural that we would have tuned out the messages of our physical selves. These are the voice of our bodies, the means of connecting deeply to this physical experience. However, as sensory disconnection was primarily enacted from our sub-conscious we did not realize the penetrating internal separation we were creating or how it would simultaneously repress our own Divine awareness into a long extended dormancy. Now, as we reinitiate the interactive flow between our awareness and our senses, we reclaim an important link to living a fully expressed life. In the same action, we release our inner wisdom to flow freely and to bless us fully.

As we play in renewed connection to our senses and all they offer, there is yet another gift we will effortlessly rediscover: Free Will Choice. We have each heard of this, spoken of it, and been aware of its existence—conceptually. Unfortunately, that is the extent to which we have given ourselves and each other permission to express this powerful blessing. We can witness the truth of its absence in our world through the unlimited and often unrelenting presentations of judgment that dominate virtually every area of life on Earth.

Authentic Free Will Choice is the clear understanding that another's choice—although it might differ from ours—is the absolute correct choice for them. Within a Free Will realm, how can it be anything less? We are the only ones, as individuals, who can know what choice offers the greatest potential for our life experience. This does not mean we will always know how to choose what is most gentle. There are occasions when the challenges we inadvertently invite into our lives are exactly what will produce the most growth. Whatever our personal choice may be in any moment and whatever the result, rekindling Free Will Choice as a living, active presence begins with maintaining our ability to not agree, without sliding into the judgment of disagreement with any other or their actions. As we begin applying the ways through which we can extend this universally given freedom to others, both the message and responsibility of that sovereignty settles into our own multi-levels of consciousness. Judgments of ourselves, those known consciously and those hidden deeply within, begin to fall away as pieces of the foundation upon which those judgments have been dependant, begin to crumble.

All judgment is an active denial of Free Will. It is the primary means by which we restrict our own and oppress another's. All lack of self-trust is based in judgment; therefore, it also overrides Free Will. Therein, self-judgment and a lack of self-trust are two faces of a single coin, each resulting in self-condemnation that immediately provokes self-distancing, suppression of the senses, disassociation from the body and the moment. Thus each dilutes our experience of living. Because this is a circle that always feeds directly into itself, we can observe and have long been living the same connectivity from the opposite perspective. Distancing from the moment, the senses and from life is rooted in an absence of self-trust. This results in an expansion of both self-judgment and externally projected judgment. Judgment—in any form—offered in any direction—restricts one's expression of Free Will Choice. To set down any one of these life-restricting traditions disrupts the continuity of the pattern, offering a clear path to peace and richness of life.

Mental Chatter

Have you ever wondered how to stop the raging tide of thoughts running through your mind, exhausting you through confusion and anxiety? Have you wondered just exactly what is so different about those people who seemingly manifest inner peace through hours of meditation, prayer, yoga, and other various well-known practices, while you continue to retrace old patterns of self-question and doubt? Are the continuing questions of what, how, why and where all too familiar antagonists? Each of these are illustrations of the tormented state from which our minds have struggled to function.

This conflict is understandable when remembering the opposing stories we have each heard throughout our lives. One history speaks of us as having been born of and imbued with Divinity. On the other hand, we are also said to be exiles from a previously exalted state. Thus leaving the impression that being incarnate is similar to attending a school for the spiritually remedial.

Even if not consciously engaged in these stories, they remain an element of each of our cellular and genetic memories. Everything carried within the body as memory, whether conscious or unconscious, has an active effect on our mental processes and therein, our lives. Representations of each of these story-induced thoughts can be witnessed throughout our world today. Reviewing our religious teachings, societal traditions, spiritual viewpoints and even world political perspectives, we see this pattern of mental unrest expressing itself, liberally.

What, how, why and where did the mind become bound within this state of inner conflict? With the re-emergence of our own Divine expressions, these queries have little genuine value to us. What *is* essential to understand is how to soothe, calm and assure our dear minds. Certainly there are ample teachings and processes that speak about transforming, processing or releasing our mental conflict. If it were truly this simple, wouldn't we have all done so long ago?

The one thing that is rarely, if ever, mentioned is befriending our mind. Certainly this is not an invitation to follow along on its endless wanderings, first this way and then in that direction. We have each spent countless hours on these rambling rides, each resulting in little more than complete exhaustion.

As our mind initiates any stream of conflicted chatter, it is clear our attention is being requested, demanded even. Often too, is our acquiescence being sought. Typically our response has been one of anguish, an exact mirror of what our mind is expressing. With the rallying back and forth of the many opinions, opposing perspectives, recommendations and suggestions that toss to and fro, we have habitually struggled to just silence the commotion. Sometimes by trying—desperately—to make what we judge as the right choice. On other occasions, we attempt a diplomatic stance within the clamor that is racking our mind.

What we consistently forget is that whatever choice we do make, our mind will continue to offer from its bottomless wealth of "what if's." It is simply not possible to locate a single choice that is so right as to permanently silence the mind. As to playing diplomat, this only places us at the center of the web within which the mind is flailing.

It is significant to acknowledge that; in spite of its internal restrictions, our mind has been both an important ally and our dearest friend. We communicate with our minds more than any other person or energy—in fact, we do this almost continually. It has been our own minds that have listened to us, attempted to hold our secrets, and tried with their limited power to answer each of our seemingly endless questions. Our mind has been our most prominent internal cheerleader, harshest critic, enthusiastic supporter, and boisterous detractor. Sticking with us through all the events of our days—our dear mind has played an essential role in every moment of our lives.

It is time to offer the same loyalty in return. To help your mind relax and experience true peace, stop asking it to assess and analyze each bit of minutia passing through your life. This has been a significant source of our perpetual inner torment. Set down the search for an idealized state of perfection. Embrace all that is present within each individual moment. Stop bruising your mind with unending questions in one moment, and pleading with it to, "*Please, just hush,*" in the next.

Initiating the practice of returning our mind's friendship is a powerful generosity toward healing the on-going conflict. One important realization when sincerely befriending our mind is that very often all our mind wants is to know it is heard. This does not require agreement with, participation in, or designation of rightness and wrongness. When your mind is offering from its abundant perspectives, have you ever considered responding with an uncomplicated? "Hello, I hear you." One of the greatest driving forces for all humans is to know we are seen and heard. From where would such a desire emanate? Primarily, our minds. That being so, offering this gentle gift consistently without drifting into the time-worn habit of further engagement helps the mind deescalate.

It is tremendously helpful to realize that our minds do not continue in their conflicted states out of a desire to intentionally antagonize. On the contrary, the primary motivation for the mind when winding through its endless data and offering its succession of suggestions is, to please. One of the mind's most well-guarded secrets is its quest for approval. Of course, that would be true. We each seek appreciation and the mind is the point from which a majority of this is generated. Our mind has as much love—self-love—as our heart, liver or any other part of our being. Since this is true, it must also carry as much self-judgment, criticism and insecurity as any other aspect of our individual whole.

Certainly we are all well skilled at berating ourselves. As we self-criticize or self-judge for any choice or action, we simultaneously censure our mind. How often do you extend appreciation toward your mind for a successful result, a valuable moment of guidance or any other reason? This is not something we are accustomed to practicing. Such levels of self-kindness are not commonly witnessed. This was definitely not modeled for the vast majority of us during our formative years. Now we have the chance to practice our own creator skills by establishing new patterns of self-love and nurturance. Playing with multiple approaches of listening to, responding lovingly to, and acting in support of our own minds is an outstanding means of developing sincere patterns of personal upliftment.

Any time we begin establishing a new behavior, it is likely to require a bit of repetition. Notice any tendency to assume a tense or defensive posture. On one hand, it is natural to impulsively brace against the static battering of the mind. After all, it is a stance long practiced. From an expanding viewpoint, it is also an opportunity to relax, breathe and proceed in a new manner. You will surely have many chances to playfully experiment with this new approach. As you become more spontaneously consistent in offering gentle acknowledgment to your mind, unwavering when affirming that you are paying attention to some bit it is offering, it will calm. Your mind will begin to relax more readily. One step at a time, the former roar will be replaced by emerging moments of peace.

When there are matters that do genuinely require your attention and that do need to be addressed, you will discover an ever-increasing ability to do so with ever-decreasing mental strife. This approach will offer you, and your dear mind, more energy for the meaningful things of life, such as remembering the grocery list when leaving for the market.

One useful action while adopting this new approach to internal inter-action is to breathe. In the old tradition of feeling batted about by our mind's chatter, our muscles became tense, our breath slowed and became shallow, our attention was scattered and our emotional bodies were exhausted. In befriending your mind, you are daring to offer restoration to your entire being.

Self-Trust

All of us have experienced moments of self-doubt, insecurity, timidity, tentativeness, apprehension and any other number of unsettled emotional reactions. Each of these is merely another defining term for the absence of self-trust. Whether this internal instability lasted only a few moments or elongated over a greater time frame, the emotional trigger remained the same—the sense and belief that we were not adequate to the task, did not have the right or sufficient understanding, that we were the wrong person in the wrong place and that this would soon become publicly apparent.

A primary kindness we can offer ourselves in these moments is remembering that moments of uncertainty are natural within the physical realm. The more traditional habit is to leap to self-judgment. This only insures an undesirable, uncomfortable outcome. It is through the act of imposing judgment upon ourselves; we become the guarantors of that adverse result. Another common knee-jerk reaction is to project judgment onto whoever is offering us this challenge. To avoid the natural discomfort evoked when meeting a challenge, we convince ourselves another is intentionally trying to undermine us by exposing our lack of capacity in some area. Even if this is true, we are not required to play along. The choice is entirely ours. Do we succumb to the undermining intention—thereby becoming a participant in our own upending—or embrace the challenge, trusting ourselves to achieve a positive conclusion?

We are each familiar with these instances and emotional surges of deep, unnerving question and doubt. It is a natural part of being human. The entire reason for coming into physical form is the repeated opportunity to discover the vastness of ourselves. To do this requires bumping into the walls of our self-imagined limitations. When we embrace these moments heartily and relax into a challenge, we gain far more than what is apparent on the surface. Whether the final result is stunningly favorable or only a moderate success, the potential benefit to our self-image and self-trust for having courageously given our all is tremendous. The willingness to remain present with each and every opportunity is likewise a choice to remain present with ourselves. So many times we have run away by sinking into our troubled emotions, making them our singular focus. We have jumped into the overwhelm expressed by our mind. As we take evasive action to avoid *feeling* the fear evoked by the challenge, we mute our awareness to our physical senses and distance from the moment of *now*.

A most gentle approach to understanding the absence of self-trust with which you are burdening yourself is observing your level of expressed measuredness. Anytime you are interacting or communicating with another, *notice* how freely you express yourself. Is every word measured, weighed, shaped and re-shaped prior to delivery? How much of your focus rests on the question of how you will be received and if what you are offering will be rejected, judged or dismissed? *Notice* how tightly you hold your body while in active relationship. How much of the authentic you must remain tucked away, silenced, for fear of dismissal?

A most excellent means of understanding your commitment to measuredness is observed through your responses to unexpected shifts and changes in your day or schedule. What is your internal response when invited to take spontaneous action? Are you able grasp the excitement of the moment or does this amount of freedom feel intimidating? Is spontaneity only comfortable in specific situations or around preapproved people? And, is that true to the energy of authentic spontaneity? To what extent must everything be planned and scheduled? Most revealing is *noticing* the extent to which your mind produces—what appear to be—reasonable justifications for needing to maintain rigorous scheduling of each hour in the day and to incessantly live exclusively from pre-designed scripts or outlines?

Life is meant to be an adventure of wonderful surprises. This is the promise of being in physical body. If you are restricting yourself to only that which is written on your calendar, you are expressing a distrust of both yourself and life. Again, do not scold yourself. Release any temptation to *force* yourself into a different pattern. After all, it would be just that—another pattern with a different chart or diagram. *Notice*. Surprise and spontaneity are different faces of the same experience. Simply *notice* your aversion to being surprised, to acting spontaneously. *Notice* the internal reaction to any suggestion of deviating from what is orchestrated. *Notice* if you project judgment upon the one who suggested that departure from the pre-written program.

As you play with *noticing*, do just that. *Notice*, and do not judge. *Notice* and do not immediately shift to an alternate demonstration of measuredness. *Notice* what you are experiencing through your senses. *Notice* the center of your body, that space surrounding your primary organs. Are your muscles tight, or at ease? *Notice* if your breath is shallow or deep and effortless? *Notice* if your mind is silent and attentive or rambling on with editorial advisories? The amazing result of doing nothing more than *noticing* is a spontaneous decrease in the measuredness with which you restrict yourself. Developing a practice of *noticing* supports you to naturally remain in presence with yourself. Doing nothing more than remaining present, ceasing to abandon yourself is, in itself, an act of self-trust.

We will never move past the time-worn tradition of mistrusting ourselves by trying to uproot it. What we focus on expands. If we focus on the absence of trust and focus on the fear, it grows. Remaining gently present with ourselves, *simply noticing* re-aligns our attention and places us in the center of the moment we are experiencing. On the occasions when you realize, retrospectively, that you did not remain present and did not *notice* your awareness drifting, let that be okay. Do not leap to self-recrimination. You will only add fuel to the previously raging and now diminishing fire of doubt, of not trusting yourself. Give yourself permission to be "fully" human, which does not mean "merely" human. Your humanness is in no measure a state of "less than." This old belief has been key to sustaining our self-judgments and fueling our absence of self-trust.

There will always be more days, more conversations and more challenges. Some days you will remember to remain fully present with your experiences. On other days you will drift through the minutes and at the end wonder where the day went. Each of these days, moments, and experiences is of equal value. Both are carrying you forward in the continuous discovery of your complete self.

Trust exists only in the *now*. Silent calm of mind exists only in the *now*. The messages delivered from our senses can be heard only in the *now*. Free Will Choice is empowered only within the *now*. Our connection to our inner wisdom is realized only in the *now*. Embracing all we are, just as we are, takes us out of judgment, which is perfection driven. This self-embrace gently sets us back into the moment—into the calm, centered peace that is natural to us—when we cease to judge, distance from, measure and direct, argue with, or endlessly question ourselves.

This time in our collective evolution is—in and of itself—the invitation to practice self-trust until it is our all-encompassing reality. As we use our power of choice to *notice* the multitude of reasons that exist for embracing ourselves, we begin enjoying being who we are and the life we are living. This single shift of focus will transport us into a completely fresh and new internal reality which naturally flourishes into an expansively supportive external reality.

Understanding Structure

O ur struggle to claim an invigorated self-image has been deeply complicated by the absence of self-trust expressed by our conflicted minds. As a result we abandoned the power available only through practicing unrestricted Free Will Choice. These internal self-abandonments drove us to look to the external world for personal definition, a sense of safety, comfort and evidence of correct action. Essentially we have been searching for something visible and tangible after which to model ourselves, our lives and our actions. Thus was born the age of structure. Committed to an idea that we dare not trust ourselves we collectively created inflexible rules and specific guidelines for how to live and who to be. In our dedication to this pattern we constructed ruling bodies through which to monitor each other's adherence to each nuance of imposed regulation. We have vigilantly watched each other, always judging what we label right, wrong, good or bad action.

Structures of society, politics and religion were created and have continued to expand their ruling power. Each offering additional instruction in what we judged to be both proper and improper deportment of our personal beings. We enacted endless regulations to insure communal well-being. Structures of idealized behavior and personal presentation were established as models from which to live. That labeled *good*, we mimicked and often ordained as law. When deeming something or someone *bad* we leapt to condemnation. Within this system *bad* was most frequently nothing more than stepping outside the pre-illustrated lines of a specific structure. Whether this was an individual judgment or one of the myriad forms of community endorsed 'witch trials' instigated over the generations, the result was the same. We repressed our internal truth, illegalized our sparks of personal uniqueness and opted for a more robotically ordained set of actions and personal presentations. Structure upon structure was instituted, each ultimately claiming to be the great gatekeeper of essential protection and enhancement.

What we chose to overlook was how the illusion of self-protection served as the driving force within each structure. We imagined this protection as being from each other. However, lacking basic trust for ourselves, we had no overflow from which to share with another. So ultimately these structures were implemented as a protection from what we feared seeing or feeling of and within ourselves.

From the Inside-Out

One of the more damaging effects of structure is also the very reason for which it was founded. In order to follow the life map as detailed by structure we were forced to view our lives and, in fact, our entire beings from the outside-in.

From one perspective this approach was of great relief to each of us. Within our question of self-value, we lived in constant doubt of our every action, our every choice. To varying degrees, this remains true. Having a single body of guidelines—we were able to mold ourselves to that which the collective community had ordained as appropriate. We had an exacting list of criteria by which to avoid our 'bad' selves. Since 'bad' included everything not pre-ordained by the reigning structure, this system functioned as a suppressant to our uniqueness. In spite of the conscious adherence to structure, our authentic selves, our Divine selves continued to speak to us, to love us, and to offer us unwavering support. It was only natural that we would experience moments of leaning into this more uplifting presence, thereby temporarily rejecting the limitations of structure.

These contradictory expressions of living provided the foundational ingredients for the argument within which our minds still wrestle. To be good, follow all the rules, and therein, be accepted by the collective. Or, to be authentic and feel the freedom that is our natural inheritance. To feel the love that continually flows toward and through us. To this day, our minds remain troubled, repeatedly engaging in an internal tug-o-war over this very choice.

Because everything we experience within is projected outwardly, our peripheral world is but a mirror reflection of what rests within our individual selves and collective whole. Therefore all structure is an out-picturing of the internal separations, restrictions, and distorted imaginings held within our minds. Subsequently, the only way to realize and actualize our individual authenticity is to live from the inside-out. Structure is a precise illustration of how we look to our world to define us from the outside-in. This has resulted in an obsessive need to mold all who inhabit our world to the patterns of our personally adopted doctrines and parameters. Under these dictates, doing nothing more than playing in discovery of our individuality is feared as an intention to actively subvert the prevailing structure. Thus, non-compliance is the fuel of all our wars, ancient and current, religious, social and political. All manners of abusive behavior ranging from hate crimes to ostracizing a neighbor with the 'wrong' color hair are a result of the judgment ignited when one dares to express their individual distinctiveness.

In authentic presentation we are an equal partnership of Divine and Human presence. Our Divinity rests within the center of our beings. As it rises through our cells it joins in actualizing partnership with our human self, from the inside-out. The greater portion of what is known by us rests in our unconscious and subconscious. As we grow and expand these unseen levels feed our conscious awareness, from the inside-out. Our emotions are an electro-magnetic flow which stimulates us, from the inside-out.

The principle purpose in creating massive structures was to shield our surface layers of awareness from what rested most deeply within. We used structure to turn our personal universes upside-down. We actively created a means by which to shift out of the organic flow of living from the inside-out, by looking to our *outside* world as a model for definitions *in*to which to fit ourselves. All this in avoidance of the condemnation that we feared *might* rise from the inside-out. Remembering that the imagined—inevitable—reproach is the by-product of our ancient myths of being exiles, we see that this is just one more structure through which we have self-imprisoned. The paradox being; we attempt to avoid the pain of inner condemnation by sentencing ourselves to the agony of internal separation. We avoid imagined punishment by battering ourselves to remain small enough to fit the limited self-expression sanctioned by structure. What a silly—albeit excruciating—game we have been playing with ourselves. Fortunately, you cannot move the air in only one side of a balloon. Consequently the moment we begin understanding structures patterns, the seams spontaneously begin to unravel.

Structure is intentionally applied separation. It is an active choice to avert our attention from and dull our senses to the voice of our authentic self. We place structures dictates and ideologies between our outer selves and inner selves, always requiring that the inner mold and shape to the outer. Essentially, we have erected walls between ourselves and ourselves.

Then there is the havoc all this has reaped upon our dear minds. The conflict through which our minds continuously circle is separation in action. It is the mind expressing inner conflict while continually struggling to determine which voice to follow, which guidance to believe; the gentle presence of our inner wisdom or the outer laws of the prevailing structure.

The act of *noticing* is a supremely gentle way to support our mind and offer freedom to our Divine essence in its reawakening. This same practice simultaneously returns us to a natural flow from the inside-out. Through structure we have already participated in enough 'doing to' ourselves. Now simply *notice* when your internal preference is one thing and your mind is directing you to an alternate path, likely one traditionalized by structure. Then choose. Do not force anything. The world will not cease to turn on its axis if, in this single moment, you opt to proceed along the path of structure. Initially you may witness yourself choosing structure in multiple situations.

However, as you progress through your days—*noticing*—you will also experience yourself naturally drifting away from structure's rigidity, with increasing frequency.

Through the uncomplicated, force-free act of *noticing* you are re-claiming tremendous levels of responsibility in your life. The primary reason structure has sustained dominance for so long is our individual and collective commitment to self-distancing. The antithesis of *noticing*. Each time we *notice* an opportunity to make a choice, whatever trajectory we pursue, by actively choosing—anything—we re-empower ourselves. *Noticing* re-connects us to the inner universe of our individual beings. It reminds us of our uniqueness and reminds us that our uniqueness is a gift to both ourselves and all those around us. For long enough we have hidden our individuality from ourselves and each other. Uniqueness, individuality were contradictions to everything for which structure was created. Now we are ready to remember the most important truth about structure. It is our creation. We dreamed it, implemented it, and empowered it to the point of forgetting that we are its designers. Structure is now the reminder of how we opted to apply our Free Will Choice—in an earlier time. In this moment we have the freedom to make the choice, to choose anew.

The Perfection Paradox

By its very nature—structure is staid, rigid. However glancing back over the many generations and their evolving ethos we witness expansions and progressions within, even if not elimination of, the established structures. Even structure has self-expanding underlying forces. One of the most poignantly apparent being the driving compulsion, quest, need to perfect. Our ancient myths have compelled each succeeding generation to seek a vision of personal perfection, by painting us as refugees striving for release.

Let's first view the perfection paradox from one of its most obvious demonstrations; the quest for perfection of our physical forms. The extent to which we have condemned our bodies has spawned an inter-connected series of multi-billion dollar industries.

We express this most exaggeratedly in the western hemisphere. In one moment we guard and protect our bodies jealously. With the very next breath, we pick them to pieces.

Another demonstration of living from the outside-in is how we maintain a constant vigil for physical flaws that will surely reveal our undeniable inner failings. We feed and inflame our commitment to this belief from deep within our primal level, to the surface of our consciousness. Compulsively, we seek out new approaches to improve and perfect. Our dear bodies are alternately starved into unnatural thinness, then expanded to uncomfortable size by being fed substances devoid of nutrition and full of unhealthy fats and chemicals. We follow-up with surgical reshaping, and then camouflage our dear selves behind endless adornments. All the while we are filling them with the self-defeating energy of unrelenting criticism.

It is an interesting paradox we have created. We claim to know that we are beings of vast intelligence, wisdom, love, compassion and insight. Simultaneously we bludgeon ourselves, particularly our dear bodies, only to be shocked and horrified when they listen to our de-valuing messages and respond by presenting irritation, impatience, sadness, a lack of personal fulfillment or even great physical illnesses into our lives. With the onset of any of these experiences, our driving need to perfect is further agitated. And so the vicious—self-created—circle continues to turn.

The mal-treatment of our bodies is but one example of our quest to perfect. Certainly we can see this in many areas of life. Whether our individual choice is to badger ourselves toward perfection through a chase for finance, social affiliations, political associations, our choice of spiritual studies, or academic achievement, or the way we demonstrate our willingness to subvert our own well-being to the care of anyone who wanders down the street, it is all the same. The hunt for perfection is the attempt to prove our worthiness to those in our outside world so we can feel justified in claiming it for our inside world. Since the reality of our lives is that they are inside-out experiences, this goal is unachievable. Thus, our commitment to perfection is the root to most pain we have experienced, via self-inflicting, as well as the distress we have projected upon others. Further, perfection seeking actualizes the quest for an ever-elusive, non-existent, while clearly specific, destination.

The time has come that we *must* set this habit down. Everything in our world is pointing to the certainty that our structures have become so top heavy and burdensome as to hazardously limit our lives, internally and externally. This is evidenced through the increasing rages of disease, widespread hunger, and an excruciating lack of emotional fulfillment within billions of our dear brothers and sisters.

There is only one solution to this epidemic. Embrace yourselves—just as you are. This is not an invitation to pretend to embrace that for which you do not—sincerely—feel love. Begin exactly where you are in this moment. Actively appreciate everything you already recognize as being wonderful within yourself. When encountering a judgment, *notice*, without inflaming it with further endorsement and just move on to the next moment. These specific actions re-align you with living from the inside-out. As self-appreciation becomes a habitual practice, the old self-criticisms organically dissolve from the space they formerly inhabited. In this exists vast potential for personal freedom.

Imprisoning ourselves behind our desks, checkbooks, datebooks, itineraries, hiding within our carefully selected group of pre-approved associations has been a wicked game of perfection seeking. A brutal self-abuse repeatedly inflicted upon ourselves. Our belief in our imperfection has created and sustained great internal separation. As with all things in life, we have projected this separation onto our outer world. What exists within will be expressed without is the natural and unchangeable pattern of our world. To the extent we still demand perfection of ourselves, we remain only guardedly inter-active with the greater representation of humanity. This has long been our primary means of hiding our supposed imperfections from others, and most significantly from our own acknowledgment.

The quest for perfection is a sneaky and never satisfied thief of both time and vigor. Only by reclaiming all the energy otherwise, wastefully, expended in pursuit of perfection do we have sufficient to share in more collectively supportive endeavors. The degree to which a dream of perfection has created a tunnel-vision of self-focus is one of the more derisive aspects of the perfection paradox. As we actively participate more broadly in all of life, we no longer have time to focus so entirely on ourselves. We lose all interest in chasing that same old carrot. Instead we discover the exhilaration known to those who do share freely, openly, unapologetically of their time, energy and their personal presence. Deep penetrating satisfaction is the gift we give ourselves when allowed the freedom to be out front and present with all of our brothers and sisters. Not just those pre-screened, but all who grace our path. Thus the quest to capture perfection is spontaneously replaced by a celebration of the uniqueness already living within each of us.

Personality and Asserted Identity

By setting aside the quest for structure sanctioned perfection we give ourselves the opportunity to discover our true inner harmony. To relax into this realization let's unveil two of the more pervasively self-undermining structures erected. These two are powerfully instrumental in sustaining distance from our authentic selves which is the introduction point to inner peace. Additionally they are both mighty supporters of and thoroughly dependent upon the perfection paradox. The two; Personality and asserted identity. We designed these constructs as keepers of the great well of stories we have written and depended upon to tell us who we are, what we fear, and what our preset reactions to life *need* to be.

These structures defend our minds perplexed state so radically that we have come to view our fears and turmoil as personal truths. In reality, they are nothing more than beliefs and ideas. Nevertheless our dependence on these stories successfully molded them into structures of behavior and personal presentation. Even now, our conflicted minds are committed to listening for warning signals evoked by fear.

We wholly believe these alarms will protect us, are our only protection. In actuality, all any fear does is help sustain the veils shielding us from the truth of who we are, the truth of anything. Fear sustains inner separation. That is its job. It assures our focus will continue to flow from the outside-in. At our most transparent, we are powerful, limitless beings. However our distrust of ourselves in wielding that freedom is so intense that we developed structures—personalities, asserted identities which generate endless volumes of beliefs, and ideas as a means of hiding from both ourselves and all others.

In developing these structures, we have not only *not* remained safe, we have actively disassociated from the natural ease that exudes from our internal magnetic center. These structures are the creation of a confused mind, struggling between the calm voice of our inner self and the ancient myths of our fundamental incorrectness. They present a series of doctrines, dictates and a requirement of uniformity in behavior. Personality and asserted identity are the actualization of condemnation of uniqueness, and through all this set the mind to its impossible destination-driven pursuit of perfection. All structure is strict and unforgiving in detailing everything that rests outside the parameters of perfection. Which is also to say, that it offers little clear understanding as to what does qualify as perfect. This is one of structures great holds to power. Demanding that which cannot be identified, thereby understood. Subsequently its parameters are ever-transient, therein unquantifiable and so—consistently unattainable. The only absolute in acquiescing to the demands of structure, the structures of personality and asserted identity, the structure of perfection seeking, is a continuous absence of inner peace.

Experiencing ease while our mind continues the pursuit for perfection, are mutually exclusive experiences. At this point in our evolution, the structures of personality and asserted identity—as with all external structure—have already begun sliding into disintegration. To actively participate in furthering this progression, let's understand the specific function of each.

Personality is our self-imposed blueprint of who we want to envision ourselves as being. It includes input from both our cellular and genetic memories, combined with the definitions and influence offered by those around us, then adopted as our own. Completing the image we combine this with the lingering effects of our personal choices and weave them into our individual visions of arriving at the destination of being a perfected self.

The personality is who we want to shape, mold and—as is often the case—bully ourselves into being. Yet if it is constructed around what we want to see, must it not also be a cylinder of protection from what we most fear, what inner truths and illusions we struggle most diligently to hide from ourselves?

At its foundation, the personality does offer significant personal insight. Unfortunately in lieu of an unwavering self-image it is left to exaggerate or mutate those potentially clarifying images. The end result being a composite of our true self camouflaged behind the prevailing fear of our ever-so-merely human selves. A powerful action in allowing the fear to melt away is releasing our longing to become perfect in the judgment-driven eyes of the collective structure.

A powerful starting place is being bold enough to speak and act authentically and transparently. Do the unthinkable. Give yourself permission to make a mistake, quote a fact incorrectly, mis-step in expressing your feelings. Most importantly, *live* this permission. Simply saying it is so, while continuing in old patterns will only compound the internal pressure. Be willing to be a human, an authentic, transparent human who is learning who you are in each new moment. If you live only by script, censor your mistakes before you have the opportunity to feel and experience them, you do not live a life. You live a diagram of a potential life. This is the function of the structure of personality; To *be* the diagram. Cease to take yourself so seriously. Stop moving through life tentatively—as if it is a constant series of passings or failings. Who are you? Dare to discover the ever-changing, ever-expanding truth of this over and over again in each new moment of *now*.

Personality's companion structure, the asserted identity, is the carefully scripted image we project outwardly. What we hope others think of us and how we want them to perceive us. Recognizing the asserted identity is who we want to be seen as, delivers the clear message that it is absolutely not who we believe ourselves to be. As with personality, the asserted identity is a mask—another construct, shaped by the drive to perfect. At the very least it is designed to project an *image* of perfection, even when it is an image in which we ourselves hold no confidence. Asserted identity is just that, an assertion of an illusory identity, created to restrict others from seeing our true self—or more pointedly, who we fear our true selves to be. It is one of our habitually utilized tactics for sustaining separation within ourselves, our lives and from others of our world. Understanding the role of asserted identity is easy when viewing its multiplicity. We have the face we show to our family members, a different one for our co-workers, yet another we push forward when meeting someone new, and the list goes on. Our asserted identity[ties] are born of our perceptions of what we lack, our impression of being personally deficient. These are the imitations we send into any situation so that the sincere and what we believe to be lacking self can remain protected—well hidden in the background. As we assert various projections of who we want others to believe we are, we lock ourselves into roles we must continuously maintain. This serves only to further deflate our self-perceptions.

We guard these pictures—each drawn through word and action—jealously, lest they become undone by a careless slip of the tongue or an action that more closely resembles our authentic, or what we imagine as our ever-so-flawed, selves. As we struggle vigorously to avoid exposure we anxiously guard the fears on which these falsified identities are founded. When a misstep inadvertently unmasks our authentic self, we scramble nervously to undo, or re-conceal that unsanctioned level which has recklessly wandered out of hiding. This is all orchestrated by our commitment to our illusioned imperfection and unacceptable nature. As loyal subjects to the dictates of the perfection paradox we have not dared to hope that what is authentic and true of us is also brilliant and amazing. It has never occurred to us that courageously unleashing our authentically transparent self might also be a great gift to others. That stepping into transparent authenticity could extend permission to those around us to set down their self-judgment has flitted beyond the scope of our imagination.

On those occasions when the personality or asserted identities have slipped into a momentary dormancy—allowing our authenticity to reveal itself—what is witnessed is our vulnerability. In the quest for perfection we forgot this great power of unification that lives within each of us. Only through exposing our natural vulnerability do our hearts reveal themselves. Forgetting this power—was essential to sustaining the asserted identities.

The perfection paradox was instrumental in teaching us to fear vulnerability. It is imperfect. Vulnerability makes us weak. Or so the mind tells us as it hurriedly struggles to re-focus our attention toward perfection seeking and destination questing. Because we have adopted this tale as a personal truth we work to tuck our vulnerability away. We strive endlessly to keep it secretly hidden—especially from ourselves. We have completely forgotten that vulnerability is the soothing balm that will heal us from the inside-out. Releasing our fear of ourselves, requires being vulnerable to ourselves. After all, it is ourselves from whom we have worked the hardest to hide. Another paradox.

Only as we set down our driving desire to always present a perfect face, offer the perfect words, display the perfect actions, do we open to the possibility of being just as we are. This is the boldest adventure we have ever undertaken. The possibility of discovering ourselves and realizing who we are is indeed worthy cause for mighty celebration.

Retiring Our Stories

Oh, how we depend on our stories. What would we ever talk about if not for the things that have happened to us—the hardships we have endured, and the pains we have survived? The treacherous paths we have traversed in order to accomplish. What would be our point of reference for how to react to any particular event or occurrence? How else would we express just how victimized or betrayed we have been—by life, our employers, our friends, our family, by God?

And if we are going to look at how we have been betrayed by God, by karma, by the universe, then we must look to the fact that we are on this physical plane, a place rife with disappointment, with challenge. How did we end up here?

Additionally, our physical form requires specific care for which we often lack complete understanding. It can become ill in ways we may find difficult to define and resolve. Our stories regularly retell of complications this situation has presented into our lives or other lives we have witnessed.

What is also true is that only by having a body do we experience the blessing of both sensory and emotionally-based sensation. Only within a physical life is this gift even possible, and oh how we struggle to subvert its effects. Further, our bodies are our clearest mirror of the freedom we give ourselves to express as our authentically transparent selves. Simultaneously they offer precise images of our fears, and how we employ those fears to sustain internal repressions and separations.

To the extent that our bodies are relaxed and we move fluidly, if we fall into peaceful slumber at night, as our elimination system functions regularly and gently, we can trust that we are allowing ourselves a state of ease. When we find any of these areas challenging or uncomfortable, our body is telling us that our emotions are blocked, in resistance or restricted.

When we notice an issue in our bodies function, rather than tracking the time-old traditions of ignoring it, medicating it into silence, stilling it through addictive behavior, or just becoming resolutely frustrated, consider speaking directly to the challenge. Settle into a quiet comfortable position. Acknowledge the troubling area. Feel the sensations that emanate both from and throughout. Feel the rest of your body. Breathe. More breathing? As you play with your breath—consciously—you will likely be amazed at how shallow it generally flows. Intentional breathing—in no structured pattern— just being aware of doing so, oxygenates the body much more richly.

Oxygen is essential to physical ease. As you relax, a broader image of what is plaguing your body will begin to form. From this will emerge enhanced understandings of the contributing mental and emotional factors. You may become aware of the triggering event from an enhanced perspective.

Since the mind is still actively conflicted, the first thing you are likely to hear is *its* voice. Listen to what it has to say without becoming engaged. As with all the new practices we develop in life, this will require repetition. Rather than considering this an indication of personal short-coming, embrace it as an adventure into self-revelation. This approach allows your mind to receive more oxygen and subsequently it calms. When you acknowledge your body as more than a nuisance, as a voice that is speaking to you through its aches and pains, a new relationship of discernable communication emerges.

Remembering transparency through active, flowing inner communication each of our levels relaxes and expresses their individual functions more gracefully. Insight to the stories we have hidden within our minds and emotional bodies is organically revealed. Healing becomes a natural and on-going experience, merging deeply into the fabric of our lives.

While we do hold dear the stories of our joyous times—our moments of shared laughter, and our precious exchanges with a loved one—all too often it is the other stories that dominate our conversations to vex our minds. The stories of our trials and the moments during which we felt deeply betrayed or persecuted are often revisited. Long past occasions when we felt pointedly unprepared or fundamentally ill-equipped for what was asked of us, continue to stir reactions to life's current circumstances. Remaining committed to these dear old stories, inspires constant dread of similar outcomes in new situations. Accordingly we restrict ourselves to limited and outmoded behaviors. Our loyalty to these dreaded potentialities becomes a succession of negative prayers.

Since time has progressed and the world is a different place today than it was yesterday, and we too have moved forward, all outcomes to each opportunity presented must reflect this evolution. In other words, holding fast to a belief that our stories are a clear map of what will, what must, ultimately occur over and over again is a refusal to allow any new wisdom gained to take root by expressing itself. Ultimately, clinging to our stories is another expression of self-directed distrust—an unwillingness to trust that we are continually growing and expanding. Commitment to the stories evidences a belief that we are incapable of creating new and different outcomes in any situation. Our stories are the road maps for repeatedly taking the same action while always expecting a different result.

The expectation itself is the promise of the unpleasant outcome. Expectation is a manner of choosing and we are ever in possession of Free Will Choice. That being so, exchange the habit of expectation for the practice of *noticing*. Give yourself space to discover who you are—truly—rather than depending on the stories to dictate who you must be.

Although we like to pretend otherwise, our stories are not who we are. They are the remembrance of experiences offered to us by life. Our stories also reveal the choices we made during those past moments, each of which is a reflection of what we were then willing to allow ourselves. Typically the stories illustrate our continuing struggle to live from the outside-in, while chasing a destination of perfection, and the consequent discomfort generated. Each of these occurrences also offered vast opportunities for growth. However the growth is only exponential to the degree we, set down the fear induced by the story, and revel in the experience of the moment. Thereby we receive the insight that has been long-available while actively avoided.

To embrace the internal expansion available, *notice* when you feel the old familiar and undesired fear rising. *Notice* the fight or flight impulses raging and, instead of running, just breathe. *Notice* what sensations you experience when you actively breathe into your center? *Notice* what is honestly occurring in *this* moment? The very act of *noticing* lifts you out of the past, out of the story, and settles you into the moment of *now*. This initiates dissolution of the energy long-carried by the story. As any of our cherished stories disperse—fade into the past—leaving only the imprint of the wisdom gained, all pain and memory of trouble or strife becomes instantly resolved, opening space to experience a more authentic expression of ourselves.

Each story retained as a point of self-identification continually distances us from our authentic selves, our innate wisdom. Maintaining any story as either something we are destined to live and relive, or as something to avoid and against which to guard, are commitments to operating from an outmoded tradition.

Dissolving structure invites us to release all the old stories. An easy approach begins with looking into how we still rely on these to define who we are. The way we continue to draw the marrow from each of them is a commitment to self-restriction. No longer clinging to structure as warnings of potential future hardship gives us the freedom to move forward unencumbered.

The gift of each story is how it details the placement of the fences we have erected in our own lives, the lines outside of which our crayons are not supposed to color. What stories of past occurrences do you hear yourself telling and re-telling? What self-image does this story portray? Strong? Victimized? Compassionate? Devalued? This is *your* dated idea of *yourself.* There are many practices that speak of letting go of the stories by forgiving those involved. How about simply forgiving yourself for forgetting to notice how much wisdom, strength, awareness and personal balance you gained through this— possibly uncomfortable—past experience. In that single acknowledgment you give the story permission to become itself—a memory—a part of the past no longer dictating what *will* be.

Transcending Judgment

Judgment is integrally connected to and almost wholly supported by our stories. The same stories that serve as our self-definitions, telling us who we are, why that is, and what we *should* fear—of both ourselves and life. Judgment is our justification for believing our lack of perfection and so serves as our primary fuel for driving the search for that ever-elusive destination. We implement judgments as monitors to self-indicate what is safe and what is not, when we are acceptable—nearing perfection—and when we are severely lacking. Ultimately, every judgment we carry or project is rooted in this— story-based, perfection seeking, destination driven—foundation.

Some occurrences within our daily movements and interactions are so startling to our psyche as to sear into our minds. These moments register somewhat like scar tissue. When some future happening appears to be shaping itself in an uncomfortably familiar and oh-so-imperfect pattern, these memory-induced fears spontaneously flood our entire being. Defensive postures are immediately adopted within our bodies, minds and emotions. It is as if these memories become actual facets of our personality. From the perspectives these facets hold, our conscious and sub-conscious minds collaborate to determine the actions and reactions we will extend to other people, places or situations. They simultaneously remind us of all our internal imperfections. They serve as a permanent *on switch* for the great fear of ourselves. Believing these unhealed perspectives to be indisputable proof of our insufficiency, we have maintained this system as a path to self-protection.

On the contrary, it is one of our most profoundly self-limiting practices. Acquiescing the habit of clinging to these memories— surrendering the driving urge to remain on-guard for potential pitfalls—soothes our emotional levels far more quickly, in some cases, instantly. Only in setting the old stories down, ceasing to hold them as warning banners, can our innate wisdom saturate our consciousness and spontaneously empower us. Most valuable; releasing the old ideas, deactivates the magnetic effect that draws other such unsatisfying exchanges into our lives. Liberation from both story and judgment is the only true means of concluding the repetitive cycle.

We are energetic beings. Applying the universal law of physics, this means that each experience of our life creates a new and differing magnetic reaction. Those most prominent moments—be they exciting or troubling—each generate an electromagnetic movement. Simple cause and effect. Depending on our stories for self-fortification, mires our days with negative emotional imprinting, thus magnetizing additional experiences of similar frequency. Furthermore, each time our energetic levels express themselves through our bodies—more specifically the emotional and sensory levels—our stories take on their own identity. They become a part of our energetic whole expressed as an aspect of our personality and asserted identity structures.

Sensations of regret, shame, anger, or any other variation of fear, trigger the aspects of our personalities and asserted identities terrified of revisiting these emotional experiences. Peering into life cautiously through the lens of our stories is an attempt to filter out anything we judge as—even mildly—threatening. Any person or situation that might evoke uncomfortable emotions, a story to which we are yet clinging, is quickly rejected. We do this forgetting a primary universal law. What you focus on—expands. Or in the terminology of physics—that into which you direct your focus, you feed energy. Looking for opportunities to judge, remaining alert for potential adversaries, standing on-guard for approaching pitfalls produces just that. The pit-fall of opportunities to judge and a flow of imagined adversaries. Habitually, we implement this model as a rationalization for our judgments. Judgment as a means of orchestrated self-protection is an attempt to hold life at arm's length.

Any commitment to non-receiving from one direction minimizes our ability to receive from any source. Consequently, rationalizing judgment enacts a full spectrum state of non-receiving. The paradox in this is seen though manifestation and non-manifestation of our choices. We select one thing or another. Immediately, we begin to watch in all directions for signs and indications that there is something innately wrong with our choice that we need to reel it back in like a fishing line, and make essential modifications. Following the voice of fear, remembering our innumerable imperfections, conceding to the memories of our stories—which tell of all those other times when we went astray—we reclaim the choice and begin reshaping. Moderately satisfied we offer the choice back to the flow of the universe—except for that one little string to which we had best hold on in case additional modification becomes necessary. And how will we know? When the choice does not become fulfilled, of course. We are indeed funny beings and the greater degree to which we relax into being amused, the less power fear has. The more fear that evaporates, the smaller judgments anchor becomes. With judgment receding and our willingness to delight in our imperfection expanding, all internal structures begin dissolving completely. So if we are going to use choice as a launch point for transcending judgment, how will we know if we have made a choice from trust or one rooted in fear and self-minimization? It all goes back to that one little string of fishing line. Having made a choice—*notice*—if you wonder if, when or how you will experience your desired outcome. These thoughts are the substance of that line you are yet holding. *Notice*—if you find yourself imagining how you will manage this or that if your desire is satisfied. It is a well-honed habit when imagining the fulfillment of a choice to include some level or aspect of discomfort to be negotiated.

We repeatedly turn to the personality and asserted identity, we review each of our stories for a signal of impending discomfort. The fallacy being; this affords us time to step back and reassess a situation before it has even had the opportunity to fully reveal itself. Essentially, we are reeling in, voiding, our choices. We imagine we are turning our focus to these structures as a means of self-protection from—yet un-manifest—discomfort. In all self-honesty, we are securing our judgments.

Often there was no threat of danger whatsoever. Unfortunately, our long-held judgments overshadowed our ability to trust this and we became too afraid to take a chance on something greater manifesting. Most of us have experienced occasions when taking a chance on ourselves was intimidating. Our stories and structures have taught us that change, in virtually any area or regard—is unavoidably threatening. This is a powerful support mechanism to judgment. Thus our mind is compelled by a continual need to define and analyze any change long in advance of its physical presentation.

Certainly, this pattern sits in direct opposition to receiving—fully or gently.

When you feel the initial spikes of fear, the most self-supportive action is to just breathe. Do not rush into retreat. Attempting to hide from the situation or your own emotional reactions is self-restrictive. Just stop and breathe for a moment, a day, or a week. Let the dust settle, and then reassess from a calmer space. Having established a state of ease, you can clearly, quietly determine if the threat is authentic, or just a habit based reaction.

Until now, we have not considered these gentle, restful steps that provide a greater expanse of objectivity. Instead, we have either plowed forward—ignoring any possibility that the caution is valid, therein finding ourselves in highly uncomfortable situations—or dropped away out of fear, forfeiting all opportunity for receiving potential benefit.

Both of these actions are based in reaction. Stop, breathe, and *feel* for the response that holds the greatest benefit before propelling yourself in an old and familiar re-action. Each time we react, our stories gain an expanded appearance of credibility. This only heightens their control over our life, which re-confirms our sub-conscious commitment to our absolute imperfection. We clarify how we undermine fulfillment of our choices when we understand our fear of change. Our choices manifesting easily or regularly would be a tremendous change. Since we have mistakenly identified the modes and dictates of structure as personal truth, this would upend structure in a meaningful way. It would completely incapacitate the greatest bulk of our judgments.

Judgment is based in a simple formula. If an experience registers no internal threat, no fight or flight response is announced by the primal mind and we are not compelled to judge. The presence of judgment tells us our primal level of mind is blaring fight or flight orders through our bodily systems to proclaim that we are being personally threatened, in some way or manner. The greater reality is that the threat was always within ourselves. Each story carries a threat—even if long past. Thus the story itself is the threat that activates the fear which provokes the judgment.

When you feel yourself judging—know that you have encountered an uncomfortable mirror. Some person or situation has reflected to you an action or expression—equal to one you carry internally—for which you hold self-judgment. All judgment is an outward projection of an inner condemnation. Set down the judgment long enough to realize what that mirror is reflecting. The natural and spontaneous result—both within and without—will be a shift to inclusiveness.

Since our stories are the embodiment of our self-rejection they repeatedly present as judgment of others. They run in a circle, always returning to the point of their initiation and then feeding back into themselves. As we process and reprocess any story in a self-battering attempt to wrench free of it, we concurrently silence the potential wisdom that was available. The mere continuation of the story is evidence that the judgment it generated is unresolved. A story, any story will always anchor us to the past until we relax and understand that the event was as filled with potential self-revelation as it was with distress. The only reason any level of suffering has continued is as a reminder of the blessings not yet realized. Acknowledging those inner potentialities is the awakening to a more completely authentic self. The story and all its connective judgment is put to rest. What is past is allowed to settle into the past.

We can only express our inner promise by being fully centered in the *now* of our lives. As we no longer judge the situations of our days by opening our senses to embrace them—we express love *to* who we are. This is the path of living as our authentic selves. Releasing judgment offers clarity to every experience we have known. Transparency gives us the freedom to love all the mirrors and teachers that have graced our lives. This love illuminates the truth of how every life circumstance was a step into wisdom, a movement for peace. A willingness to express inclusiveness evaporates all judgment sustaining the stories. Our mind is gifted the relief of stillness.

Stillness is what exists when our mind ceases to stand on-guard. No longer being required to hold the stories, chase perfection or self-abuse with a continuum of judgments allows the mind sincere peace. As the mind discovers the stillness, by natural extension so do our emotions, our senses, and the rest of our physical body.

We have each been seeking tranquility within our mind, peace from its continuing torment. In this quest, there have been many digressions into avoidance, just to find a single moment in which the exhausting banter was not claiming our constant attention. All expressions of addiction—drugs, sex, alcohol, work, sugar—have been attempts to escape this bludgeoning of our stories in continuous replay. Shutting down our senses by spending endless hours in front of a television or playing computer games were alternate attempts at escape. Each of these has perpetuated self-judgment. Leaving the stories to their correct placement—the past—fear of the future and its inevitable changes also dissolves. *Now* is all there is, all that has ever been. The moment of *now* is the only access point to peace of mind, heart and body.

Structure cannot continue in the *now*. It is entirely rooted in shaping for the future based on perpetual judgment of the past. Acceptance lives only in the *now*. It calmly recognizes the past as only what has occurred and is content to let the future reveal itself in its own exquisite timing. Through this willingness to let all be as it is, our mind becomes quiet, our energy level increases, our focus clears.

Owning Our Creations

Avoiding the snare of self-judgment for having created structure, particularly—personality, asserted identity, and our stories—is easy when we remember they have been faithful servants to us. In their day, they were vastly useful tools. It was these very structures that aided in propelling us forward in our desire for internal peacefulness. They have served as barometers, letting us monitor our progress, our successes, and our regressions. Each of these internal structures offered a point of identification, which allowed us to move forward, to rise into our authentic presence. Holding these outdated structures in any level of contempt, chastising ourselves for their creation or feeling we are a victim to them, only enhances their power to continue.

This is true of all levels and representations of both mental and emotional structure. Each one has provided yet another step toward remembering our authentic grace, truth, wisdom, strength and brilliance. Every structure has validated our expansion into completeness, or identified the regressions in which we have entangled ourselves.

Recognizing the value of our structures invites us to love ourselves without reservation. This is true of all the structures we have created. Appreciating the usefulness of these tools disperses temptation to judge either ourselves or any of our created structures. After all, judgment—as we now understand—only serves judgment.

It is tempting to wonder why, if we are creators—our desires do not manifest with immediate ease. Let's start with recalling that the majority of our more active creations were shaped from the outside-in. This was motivated by our fear of ourselves, our absolute commitment to imagining ourselves inextricably flawed. This is what dampened our enthusiasm for playing in Free Will Choice. Implementation of this gift is the means of creating from the inside-out. The formula is easy to follow. Non-belief in our innate perfection results in internal separation. Self-distancing chokes self-trust. An absence of self-trust produces a fear of what horror we might create if liberated to express Free Will Choice.

Reversely, as we stop relying on the personality, asserted identity and all of our stories, they each fade into their correct perspective. By settling into the *now*, flowing from one moment to the next and being fully *in* that moment, all of our internal levels naturally re-connect. Separation cannot exist in the *now*. It requires the past and future as points of attachment. Living an expression of fully connected wholeness self-trust, self-love, self-appreciation flow gently and unendingly. We instinctively begin living from the inside-out. When living from trust, as a wholly connected self, structure is dissolved and playing in Free Will Choice is no longer a scary consideration.

What an amazing potential living without structure, promises. To be able to vigorously embrace each new moment, because that is all there is. To be free to discover our unique selves because there is no external pattern, demanding our compliance. To be fully present with each individual we encounter because the long-held fears of ourselves, which spawned fears of others no longer hold power. To live from the inside-out, enlivening our wisdom, love, compassion and laughter. To live boldly as authentic transparency. To live. To live versus dancing around the edges of life in timid avoidance. What is truly amazing is that this is our authentic potentiality. This is the very image of any of us when we step outside the bounds of structure into our actuality as creators.

Does this mean that all structure must fall, that there be none left anywhere on the planet? Absolutely not. Any one of us can set down our personally held structures at any moment of our choosing. Gloriously, as this occurs, all our brothers and sisters witness the peace and enthusiasm that then naturally emerges from the inside-out as an invitation to play freely within their authentic selves.

Releasing Control

In spite of its desire to be of service, our dear mind has certainly struggled against us in a variety of ways. As we have now established, each of these struggles has been based around one primary fear—an absence of perfection. We have believed this renders us incapable of presenting the exact and only correct answer, perspective or result. In our mind's powerlessness to understand that there is *never* only one 'correct' response to any query, it repeatedly presumed a conviction of guilt upon itself, therein on us. Guilt of non-perfection and guilt of an inability to cultivate that long sought and purely illusory state.

This is the fuel that drives our mind's fear of losing control. The same fear is activated when it believes it has been unwittingly cut free from any event in life—it fears the rug has been pulled out from under it. Having come to think of our conflicted mind's voice as our own, when it fears it is freefalling, we experience the same anxiety. It is vital to remember that we create our own reality. Without this recollection we are not capable of taking full responsibility for that reality. If the rug is missing from under our feet, we were the ones who let it slip away or tossed it out. Rather than looking for someone or thing to blame, view the situation calmly and clearly. Thus we realize which fear or old story is being reinvented.

Ceasing to react to every to fear vibration emanating from the mind, is equally important. This allows us to discover that, possibly, no loss was suffered. There may be no danger looming in front of us. Sitting calmly to discern what is honestly occurring rather than jumping each time our mind does, reduces the power it has to wreak havoc in our lives. The most commonly expressed alternative; to dive and clutch for anything within our grasp, in attempt to steer the flow of life, to manipulate ourselves, those around us and the overall situation. Relax, become comfortable and allow, or grapple for control over the universe and all of life.

Energy, life force, is not linear. Life has its natural ebb and flow, much like the waxing and waning of the moon, or rise and fall of the tide. Each time our mind senses the natural ebb and flow of life expressing any exaggerated pattern, it panics. It moves into fear that it will not have the answer, not know the resolution. It experiences a spontaneous dread of its 'lack of perfection' being exposed and leaps to control life by suppressing the natural bio-rhythmic pulse.

As its internal alarms rage, it screams for you to stop, shift, do anything that may resemble self-protection. We are so accustomed to following our conflicted mind's fearful calls, we succumb to its control—even when we know we are likely to regret it.

We may experience this as a sudden loss of interest in a project or situation for which we had great excitement—just moments or days before. We commonly believe the waning enthusiasm is a sign for us to stop or hesitate. Occasionally, we imagine our project was somehow taken away, leaving us with a sensation of having been deprived of something potentially dear.

Whatever the case, when the commitment to a project has clearly diminished, it is wise to pause and breathe. Centering helps you to feel—not think—but feel the true motivation behind this shift of enthusiasm.

Control is a chief characteristic of a structure-dedicated mind, therein an approach frequently exercised by each of us. One of the simplest ways to identify control is observing your judgments. Control is completely based in the need for one item, one direction, one idea, one philosophy, or one truth to be seen as more, or better. Therein rests the assumed permission to judge everything else.

A most common practice of control is our incessant need to know. Our need for advance notice or elaborated mental understanding is always based in control and generated by a need for assurance of personal safety, a promise we are moving in the correct direction in order to perfect, in order to achieve a superior destination.

The truth is we already know everything we need to at any given moment. We possess the awareness to take any next step presented to us by life. Yes, in those next steps we will learn more. And that is the gift of those progressions. To have known in advance would have eliminated the value in having the experience. It also would have cheated us of the pure fun of discovery. The endless quest to know now what cannot possibly be known until a later day, week, or month, is a trap. It sustains internal separation, draws our attention away from the *now*. It is wholly dis-empowering. The antithesis of what our mind is attempting to achieve. Remember: Life is meant to be an adventure, a series of wondrous surprises.

Being excited to discover life fresh and new with each re-centering into *now* is a persuasive antidote to the control driven—need to know. So what if you are moving in a direction that will result in something unpleasant? If you are calm and enjoying each instant as it presents itself, you will hear your inner wisdom inviting you to gently turn left or right. However, if you are busy in your mind trying to assess each brick you are stepping on, you may miss that quiet voice. And if you do, don't sit in distress wringing your hands. Don't frivolously waste energy wondering what you did wrong, or beating yourself up for your obvious imperfections.

Challenge happens. It's a valuable ally in our lives. It adds spark and adventure that can be tremendous fun—if you are not mentally, physically and emotionally rigid with resistance. Challenge emancipates your inner wisdom—if you are not consumed by a mind-driven compulsion to control. Challenge illuminates your inner strength. Like any muscle, this atrophies if not moved and stretched. Challenge is absolutely necessary for growth. We have all chosen specific challenges and through them have expanded into more of our authentic transparency. Sincere congratulations to each of us for this courage, for making these choices did require audacity.

Unexpected challenge, uninvited challenge, the challenge that catches us completely unaware—these are some of the most enriching opportunities. They are also the ones most likely to activate our control impulses. If we relax when these arrive, remember that there are gentle choices available within any challenge; we travel the path of being enhanced *by* the unpredictability of the experience. Resting into the randomness of any challenge is a mighty act of setting down the habit of control. Breathing into the event rather than moving into 'management of' is a beautiful expression of self-trust. Each of these upends the drive created by the perfection paradox. Freedom to discover each life encounter as it arrives is restored.

Each challenge produces any number of twists and turns. Embrace the various experiences as they are, just as is revealed. There is no value in dissecting and analyzing the occurrence, looking for each scrap of hidden meaning. Make a choice, take a step. Listen with your senses. Feel the direction into which your heart is guiding you.

The habit of analyzing every possible symbology in each step through life, is an attempt to control life itself. Consequently, we look right past untold volumes of gifts that life is holding right in front of our noses. Not to worry. Nothing is ever lost. Each of those will return again and again, until we are able to relax, *notice* and receive. All of which transpires—only in the *now*.

When we calm down and live the varied presentations of life, one after another, we become alive, become life itself. As life becomes actualized within you, it is able to flow through you—express itself as you. There is no greater remedy to control than life.

We have exercised our muscle of control by trying to manage life. We have projected it onto our physical selves, our partners and families, our friends and passing acquaintances, even our environment. Ultimately, control serves only one purpose—to shield us from our own fears. At the end of the day, the only way to protect ourselves from our fears is to stop running from them, hiding from them, and to stop finding new ways to berate ourselves for their existence.

Be free to be. No definition. No list of criteria to which you must ever-so-strictly adhere. Just be, in the moment, enjoying what the *now* is offering, delighting in the discovery of you—simply being.

The End of Competition

Another notable characteristic of structure is the way it drives us to engage in competition. This practice developed in the early ages when competition was a matter of survival. It has grown and expanded, until now we have a world in which competition is a virtual sacrament. We pay individuals huge sums of money to participate in new renditions of gladiator games. Much of our television programming is focused on reality-based competitions. As per societies demand for rivalry to infect every arena, our news networks have now reduced themselves to competition based programming.

Our financial structure, political structure, and commercial structure are each based in competition. It has even spread to our religious and spiritual communities. Only if you attend this church will you go to heaven. Or only by learning this ascension technique will you be ready for the great awakening. For this you will reap karmic bonus points and for that karmic punishment.

Then there are the areas of passive competition. Those in which we compete without realizing we are doing so. Many people express a constant spiritual striving to get the ever elusive "it" in time. What time frame would that be, and who is monitoring the clock? This particular expression moves us from the internal power base acceptance of I AM to a completely disempowered question of am I.

Other passive wanderings into competition include the times we get into a car to drive to a location forty-five minutes away, while allowing ourselves only thirty minutes for the trip. These journeys are all based in competition with time, competition with traffic, competition with ourselves and other drivers. Competing to fit just one more thing into a day is something most of us do regularly. Competition is a sneaky agent. It has ingratiated itself into our lives in a myriad of ways, some subtle, others more overt.

As we engage in competition, be it large or small, we physically, mentally, emotionally, and energetically detach from the moment of *now*. This disconnects us from any support offered by our inner wisdom or inner strength. We literally turn our entire life over to our mind. As competition dominates our mind our primal memory is activated. It sends warnings throughout our physical self that we are still in competition for our lives—that our human self is not strong, wise, quick or resilient enough to care for itself, and that we also lack the necessary external support and protection. Simultaneously, competition hinders the amount of life force energy able to flow through our bodies, minds, and emotions as it shifts our energetic current out of *being* into the smothering energy of *doing*.

Could there be a more acute example of *doing* in attempt to perfect than the act of competition? We hold our internal selves in competition to match our outer world. Through the structures of personality, asserted identity and our stories we compete with our 'bad' perceptions of ourselves to reveal only 'good' images.

Fortunately, our competitions are easy to identify and disable. In whatever endeavor you are immersed, consider your level of emotional commitment to succeeding, prevailing or overcoming. *Notice* also, any commitment to perfecting. Are you depending on external gages to determine if success is eminent? If so, you have committed yourself to competition. To settle out of this pattern, relax into being with whatever each day offers. Release the compulsion to know what is coming around the next corner. Breathe ease into your belly. Allow your authentic transparency to speak up, to be present. Give yourself permission to accept whatever does transpire and to express self-appreciation for however you respond to that occurrence. These simple actions deflate the energy of competition.

Here is a simple key to noticing if competition is at play; all competition is rooted in fear of *not*—not having, not being, not achieving. The continuing dedication to acquisition is based in a fear of *not*. Any action of hording is a fear of *not*. Finance is a primary area through which fear of *not* can be witnessed. It is the fear of *not*, particularly in the area of finance, that perpetuates the belief in and practice of manifestation rituals. These practices are typically based in reaching outside of ourselves, to fill an imagined lack inside of our lives. All manifestation is focused on reshaping or redirecting energy in one way or another. Control. Competition.

In truth, there is no need to orchestrate manifestation of anything. The universe is not lacking. We are the beloved children of this universe. Anything we are willing to receive, the universe is ever-so-eager to deliver. Of course, there are just a couple of things to remember around this. We do not get to control the experience. It is not possible to receive freely while simultaneously competing within our mind, between our various internal levels, with each other.

Another common act of competition is comparison. To compare any two or more things, they must first undergo the scrutiny of judgment. We implement judgment to determine the winner of any comparison, the winner of the competition. Learning to choose from a place of either/or just for the sake of selecting—without fault finding or dreaming one outcome to be superior to another—breaks the habit of competition.

Competition is also one of our more practiced means of self-withholding. Replace any focus on competing, comparing and controlling with the energy of gratitude. Feeling gratitude for all that you are, right *now* in this minute, gratitude for everything already given, right here, right-*now*, completely de-fuses competition.

Surely, the area of our lives most ravaged by competition is our relationships. These are our most astute mirrors in every area of life.

They present us with supreme and limitless opportunities to become comfortable in our own skin, life, and mind. We often try to avoid witnessing the part or expression of ourselves that another is reflecting back to us. It is common for us to retreat from them while trying to convince ourselves it is surely their fault. We hold them in contempt for strongly reminding us of this one or that experience. They receive blame for doing something, anything that upset our emotional or energetic balance. Every time we project our inner upset or discomfort onto another, we are competing to hide from ourselves. We are subjugating responsibility for our own emotions and sensations.

An effortless path for releasing competition is adopting an approach of conscious gentleness with ourselves. To be gentle with ourselves in all ways and respects honors the self. When making a choice, instead of comparing, simply select what *feels* to be the *gentle* option. When navigating the complexities of relationship, opt for the movements that are *gentle* for all concerned—including yourself. Actualizing our innate *gentleness* resurrects trust and love for one's self.

That's all it takes? This is a *bold* move. Gentleness with one's self is not overtly applauded in our society. We hear others being praised for being smart, being hard workers, being selfless, even for being gentle with others. But when was the last time you heard someone congratulated for being consistently gentle with themselves?

Our authentic self always speaks in a gentle voice—is a consistently gentle and ever-available source of support. Embracing gentleness as a principal in one's life is embracing all the wisdom, compassion, strength, and peace that is your innate reality. By the same token, it is through our human self that we get to express this compassion and grace with consistency.

By establishing a clear pattern of cooperation with our self, our life force, our world, we leave no corner in our life for competition to maintain a stronghold. With the shift from competition to a full spirit of cooperation, we present a new experience of ease to our mind, body and emotions. Competition oppresses, cooperation uplifts. In the passing of competition—we rise—which allows us space, energy, and far more oxygen to inspire this sustainable vision in unlimited directions and manifestations.

Seek Nothing, Be Everything

A gentle approach to practicing the art of internal cooperation is seeking nothing and being everything. Relax the habit of turning the totality of your life over to your mind's opinions, ideas, input—and fears. Settle into *knowing*, which is the basis of internal authenticity. *Knowing* reveals our innate—albeit—long-dormant—wisdom, compassion and peace. Re-connection with this inner depth reminds us that a healthy, prosperous, joyful life is not something to become worthy of, not something for which to compete. This is the actualization of who we are when living a transparently authentic existence.

In shifting from *seeking* to *being*, no longer do we *need*, no longer do we *lack*, no longer do we long for or stretch and reach. From this level of awareness, no longer do ideas dictate our actions or antagonize reactions. As we follow the road out of *seeking* and into *being*, we make the monumental transcendence of consciousness from *thinking* to *knowing*. The unending supply of ideas produced by our mind, are replaced by the gentle ease of full-body awareness.

To our further enhancement this alleviates the restraints long placed on our physical senses. Suppressing all the messages our senses were relaying was key to compelling ourselves forward in a commitment to *seeking*. It was the roaring voice of our mind admonishing us to comply with first this structure and then the next that overwhelmed these more gentle internal messages. When we relax, breathe and feel everything passing through our body, mind and emotions we spontaneously connect with our inner truth.

Having settled into awareness of our whole selves, we no longer need to *seek* the new home we desire through the mechanics of manifestation games. Instead we *become* the vibration of that home. As we step out of our own way by settling into our internal wholeness, the ideal home, in the model neighborhood selling at an amazing price gently presents itself into our life. If it is a new job we believe will fulfill us, becoming energetically and emotionally in harmony with that new position allows it to effortlessly come into being. This standing law of our universe was succinctly stated by Albert Einstein:

> ~ "Everything is energy and that's all there is to it. Match the frequency of the reality you want and you cannot help but get that reality. It can be no other way. This is not philosophy. This is physics." ~

As you play from this new space of no more *seeking*, only *being*, there is no need at all. This is the space that allows a continuum of receiving. *Seek nothing, be everything.* Allow all the structures that were seeking, doing and controlling dependant to fade into history, and the natural pattern of each day's unfolding blessings are free to enrich.

Be Life

To open ourselves to receive continual support, all we need do is realize life is not an experience we are having. Life is who we are. At our core, we are the living frequency of life force energy, individual souls journeying through a physical reality. From both physical and universal expression, we are life itself. By entertaining that single possibility, we awaken to *Being Life.*

Becoming aware, that we are not here to navigate through, but to *Be Life* is most freeing. *Being Life* is a consistent release of everything we think we know about ourselves to recognize who we truly are. The act of *Being Life* is a shift of focus from the self-identification created by our minds to a willingness to self-discover—everyday—in each occurrence—through any nature of experience. Remembering that we only know as much of ourselves as what we have given freedom of expression to, we are emancipated to accept that in every moment of *now* we are more, we know more, we Be-come more.

We have each known at least one person who expressed the miracle of embodying life. Every time we were with this person we felt more alive within ourselves. Their joy, enthusiasm, and insuppressible spirit were beautiful and contagious. Due to the vibrant exhibition of delight with life demonstrated by these people, it is common to envision them as having fewer burdens and attributing their carefree exuberance to this enviable state.

It is far more likely that this is someone who has found the key to their own life force, and recognizes the peace-inducing effects of being centered in any single minute, day or happening. Whether they would describe their state of invigoration this way or with other language, the truth of their enlivened state is self-evident. Their very presence offers consistent opportunity to witness and experience just how addictive and contagious life is—when expressed freely.

To know this reality personally, relinquish the idea that anything *unexpected* is something to dread. We have each had passing flashes of this truth. Many times we have been offered the chance to dare to move boldly and confidently into something unknown. As we cease to dread a challenge, or anything unfamiliar, as we relax the watchful eye kept on-guard for these, as we choose to embrace each experience as it unfolds, we become the living presence of gentle resolution. This is the door to consciousness. As our mind rests, consciousness awakens easily and expansively. Consciousness is not some mystical or magical experience. It is simply a living breathing expression of *Being Life*. It is the great essential truth of who we are.

Releasing our commitment to ideas of need, lack, and complexity, formed by the mind, opens the internal doors of personal freedom. Beyond these old ideas lives a state of awake-ness, a state from which we can move forward *Being Life*.

Begin each day by opening your mind and inviting life to "show me your face." Remain open to your heart, emotions, and physical senses as you travel the landscape of your day. Honor each new discovery of how rich and full *Being Life* is. Set down the fears that lock you into patterns of control and competition. They have served you well, and are now dated and worn-out old toys. Experience the constant surprises of life by ceasing to manage its flow. Venture into the vastness of your own awareness through conscious intimacy with the visceral messages of your senses. When settled this gently within ourselves, we *become*—not just experience—the freedom that was given at the time of our original, universal inception.

Our expanded conscious awareness has been gently waiting for an invitation to live fully, to express itself completely, through the physical realm. It has been waiting to communicate its delight for life, its love for all that is, through physicality. Play with and as awakened consciousness. Let this reality of who you have always been teach you what *Being Life* truly is.

The degree to which your mind spent years and decades guiding and directing your life is the extent to which you have not yet begun to live. What an exciting prospect; completing the birthing that began many decades ago. Breathing life. Feeling the whole of you.

Celebrate with yourself, celebrate with life, and celebrate the resurrection from long exile of your Divine inner wisdom. The extent to which you acknowledge all of this as you, determines the magnitude to which you will experience life from the center of that celebration.

Part II

The Discourses

Be As You Are

We are each here on this planet to bear witness for one another. We are present to witness the vibration of love as it emanates from human to human, from life force to life force. This witnessing is what supports the life presence within each of us to flow and deepen.

To bare witness for another requires our full presence with—and our undivided attention to—what is. Through this clear focus of what another has to say, to offer, to observe, we support their settling fully into themselves. Thereby, they open more completely to the vast potentials of their own life. It is through witnessing for each other that authentic awareness is able to glide generously through our beings and thereby infuse all our interactions.

Until now, the influence and importance of witnessing has not been considered. It begins by being bold enough to remain present with any mirror shone in our direction and expands as we reflect to another a sincere vision of the self they are presenting.

So often, our human tendency is to either react to another as a sensory and emotional carbon copy of what they are emitting, or simply retreat from them entirely. Each of these are ego-based actions, and both equally rooted in fear.

If instead, we look beyond the reactions of their personality and asserted identity to witness and reflect the authenticity hidden within; this more complete self is given permission and invitation to expand. Concurrently, we cease empowering our ego by giving our inner wisdom space to express itself. This is how the act of bearing witness for each other is the stimulant most kindly supportive to all our life experiences. Witnessing carries nurturance throughout all levels of our beings by virtue of aligning our focus, attention, and energy with what is genuine versus lending credibility to the old mental and emotional structures carried by both ourselves and those we witness.

From the understanding of quantum physics, we know that the molecules of any single object, living or inanimate, do not belong exclusively to that object. All molecules in existence live in a constant state of flow, continuously transferring from one space to another. Thus they exist beyond the limitations of animate and inanimate limitation. What in one moment contributed to a pillar on a building, may now be flowing and dancing with other atoms to make up what we call *self.*

Life itself is the clear demonstration of energy, molecules, and everything they create flowing in a continuous idiom of existence. By witnessing life in its own natural flow, we cease attempting to hang on to what the mind defines as ours. Consequently, we stop clutching to life as if it were trying to escape. We have all engaged in both of these self-undermining games, each of which impedes the natural movement of our life's instinctive current. This fruitless attempt at restraint underlies all the unrest and disease we have known. The energy of our beings must be set free to express fluidly, to be unrestricted in following our own organic rhythms and patterns. This is the license to discover our greatest potential.

For just this moment, step out of all thoughts of your human identity. Drift beyond every idea of your body and out from under all restrictions of the personality. Feel, for only one instant, the visceral impression of what is—the instinctive electromagnetic flow of your energy, the fullness of your sensory awareness, the peace of your emotional presence. This is the experience of all that is authentically you in full inter-connected articulation. As each of us comes to see— and more importantly—to live this reality, versus struggling within the limited and binding personal definitions erected within our minds, our expansive *Beingness* is liberated. Thus all that we are becomes boundless. Spontaneously, considerable energy formerly devoted to internal struggle is re-directed into life-enhancing activities and interactions.

We intentionally came to this planet to experience our natural Divinity in Human expression, each one of us sharing with and witnessing for all others. That being so, the entire purpose of our presence here is to play in the world of sensory aliveness. Witnessing this exuberance in each other sparks the flame within us to inspire our inner passion fully.

Giving our passion license to weave through our senses requires nothing more than ceasing to deny any natural emanation we feel moving within ourselves.

More often, as we notice sensory or emotion based reverberations, our first impulse has been to judge their acceptability or inappropriateness. What we have determined dictated if we would let them flow and be experienced or be immediately squashed with self-rejection. In this way, we repeatedly undermined our permission to dive into life with enthusiasm by holding ourselves and all of life in constant scrutiny.

We are not on this planet to pass a test or prove personal worthiness. We have long imagined ourselves accountable to some illusive and external judge and jury. In truth, it is we who have served as both. Now it is time to retire all the criteria we have used to continue in this self-minimizing pattern.

Let's begin with supporting both our Divine self and Human self equally, by no longer pretending that one is more or better than the other. Only through our remembrance that we are both, and the freedom to encounter all that means, do we discover our most thrilling potential. This is the only path by which we move beyond the illusion of separation. When fully loving and respecting each level of ourselves equally, while living from a single flow of unity, we establish a sincerely intimate relationship with ourselves.

It is not necessary to reach or work for life force, as we once believed. We are life force. Furthermore, because we are both soul and human, that life force is constantly flowing in love and appreciation to each of our levels—mental, physical, emotional, and energetic. There is no need to intentionally bring light, or love, or healing, within. We are all of these expressions. There is no cause to reach or long for any vibrational frequency of this world. All there is to do is to **be as you are.**

To **be as you are**, accept each and every one of your natural expressions—with equal enthusiasm. This is authentic self-acceptance. Shifting from the tradition of complying with the inflexible dictates of structure into full affirmation of your inherent wholeness is expressed by listening to your heart, listening to your body, listening to your emotions. Ceasing to fear connection to the emanations of your emotions, your senses, and your body, offers ease throughout your life. This is as easy as feeling how each of these levels enlivens and enriches the others. This is the practice of *noticing* you being in active appreciation of you.

The degree to which we are fully present with and within ourselves determines the extent to which we are capable of extending loving encouragement to any other. So many speak frequently and strongly of their desire to be of service. **Being as you are** is the greatest act of service anyone can offer. To **be as you are** is to live as a fully conscious expression of Humanity. In **being as you are**, you may find yourself engaging in planetary issues, social advocacy, and community building, or quietly living an individual and peace-saturated existence. It is through our Humanity that we engage this fully with life, and in doing so, simultaneously, discover the path of our greatest fulfillment.

Only by emerging from our internal secularization, created by a constant quest for perfection, will we know the joy available when our passion is allowed to invigorate our actions. We came to be engaged in life, in community with each other, witnessing and mirroring for each other. Activate the gentle path to being fully alive. **Be as you are.** Be the Humanity that is eagerly and excitedly participatory in however many or few arenas of life feel enticingly engaging.

Life being an inside-out experience, to comfortably engage in all external arenas begins with full acceptance of our internal world. Fully empower your humanness, by *noticing* what you have struggled for more than any other thing in this life. In truth, this is what you have struggled *against*. The paradox being; if you achieve what you have struggled for—on a primal level—there is a dread that your reason for existence will suddenly evaporate. Or so the structure-driven mind has alleged and maintained within its subtle levels. The more apparent motivation being that if we create only one side it becomes a choice, and that is the power from which we have most effectively hidden.

We are the universe. If each of us is *of* the universe, the dynamic of physics would tell us that we must also be a microcosmic expression of its entirety. As soul energy, we are ever connected to that whole and so maintain access to it through our own authentic radiance. If this is true, who is there that would have the power and desire to successfully struggle against us? Our higher selves? Our guides and teachers? The universal elders? God? There are none—other than ourselves—who would engage in this struggle that continues to demoralize us with such vicious consistency.

Another primary motivation for this self-violence, of simultaneously struggling in opposing directions, is our absence of trust for the yet-unseen outcomes of our choices. Believing our physical experience a quest to overcome unworthiness, we find it difficult to relax into receiving. This is only one of the myriad ways we maintain an illusion of separation within our beings which is the perpetuation of all inner struggle.

Accepting our essential nature—by straight-forwardly acknowledging we are more than we have been willing to consider—instantaneously stimulates dissolution of a majority of the struggle—effortlessly.

The fact that we are the only ones who have ever been struggling against ourselves is a magnificent testament to the power of our beings and the power of our choice. Additionally, it is testament to the fact that only we can usurp our power. This single realization speaks volumes. Amusingly, we have each taken our struggles ever-so seriously.

As to the struggles that have most frequently and successfully haunted us, what will acceptance of those reveal about who we truly are? This is the truth we are most afraid to consider. We fear what the truth of our freedom, the truth our inner strength and wisdom, and the truth of our limitlessness, might tell us of ourselves. And then there is the great fear of potentially having to accept responsibility for being the source of the limitations, against which we have so vigorously struggled. The evidence of our fear is exemplified in the realization that were this not so, we would have long ago begun living the power of these inner truths, versus using them as a tool to wield against ourselves.

Our fear of unqualified self-acceptance rests in these questions: If our power of choice and our limitlessness are already innate aspects of us, what is our purpose? Are we not here to study and practice becoming perfect? If continuing the quest is not why we are here, then what are we to do with ourselves, our days, our lives? How will we become complete and whole if we do not unveil all the answers to each of the questions? How will we prove ourselves worthy to have grace again bestowed upon us? And the ultimate question: If we are Human by virtue of our own divine choice, why is physical experience so confusing and at times, pointedly uncomfortable?

Love in its flow is all there is, and is the substance of all we are. Now as we recall our most magnificent presence by becoming willing to consider it as our authentic transparency, we cross the threshold out of struggle into living fully, freely, boldly and richly. This is not another long arduous journey into which we are being beckoned. It is a gentle invitation to live our whole and boldly impassioned selves by simply having fun **being as we are.**

Truth, Life, Love, Humanity, Divinity are all the same. They are all the reality of who we are when we express ourselves authentically. As physically manifest beings, we can experience this by living our life exuberantly. It is time to stop peering in the corners or the shadows, for those speak only of the past. *Now* is the moment to activate our completeness and ecstasy by simply **being as we are**.

There is no personal happiness available in studying endlessly, executing extreme disciplines, holding ourselves distanced and separate or toying with any other measure of restraint. These struggles will never support us in experiencing aliveness. All we are asked to do is be *just exactly* as we are. No more judgment. No more struggle. No more self-restriction. Just **be as you are.** This means being awake, alive, present with ourselves, lucid in our senses, conscious in our moments, aware of our brothers and sisters and in vivacious support of all that is. Becoming an active presence in this world is the very adventure our souls carried within themselves when entering human bodies. We can only actualize this choice to live an adventure by remaining enthusiastically open to being surprised by life and breathing this willingness into our personal *now*. This is the reason we came to this life.

Surrender to the fulfillment of life's adventures by releasing the habit of struggle. Don't struggle to stop struggling. Just set it all down. Cease to engage. Nothing will be gained by going on a great mission in search of all the details surrounding any particular struggle, or a head-count of how many resistances you have hidden within yourself. Take only one or two breaths and recall the primary point that has repeatedly aroused your self-punishing travails. Remember what has frequently erupted into exhausting inner turmoil. Gently *notice* the trigger that has activated the all-too-familiar chaos that felt like an inescapable haunting, day after week, after month, after year.

Now yield to it. Let go of all mental and emotional commitment to any particular end result. No need to engage in concern of an undesirable outcome. Whatever conclusion presents itself, you will have finally dissolved the confinement created through fear-driven avoidance. You will have provided yourself a great new in-flow of energy with which to address any future challenge.

Take a breath and gently proceed. Be free. Everything you touch will reflect that in-flow, through the way your life expands with wonderful surprises. Welcome the boundless excitement available in being this self-empowered participant walking in physicality.

Remembering Free Will Choice

Free Will Choice is key to emancipating our beings and our lives from the cycles of repeated unrest. This was the great gift given to each of us upon entering physical life. However choice must be activated for its strength to enhance our daily experiences. It is one thing to choose to eat dinner, but until we rise from the chair and prepare a meal, it does not become a genuine choice. Rather, just another exercise of playing in our mind.

Repeatedly, we engage in actions that undermine the fulfillment of our choices. This is a habit well-honed through much practice. We do this each time we fail to set any of our desires into motion. Maybe our greatest longing is for community, but sitting alone watching television or rerunning thoughts and philosophies through our mind are continual messages to our inner selves that this yearning is only a diversion, a game designed to entertain our intellect.

Every idea, every thought that is worked and reworked while never set free to manifest diminishes the abundance of living available through Free Will Choice. Instead of becoming a reality, that thought develops as an aspect of our emotional commitment to believing *we cannot*. We cannot have, receive, be or choose with any level of effectiveness.

This energetic/emotional/psychological blueprint insures that every commitment to an idea of scarcity or limitation—in any regard—is a use of our Free Will Choice to magnetize those states into our lives. Creation of the proverbial self-fulfilling prophecy is a sport in which we are each well skilled. On the other hand, a sincere, viscerally expressed commitment to the belief in wholeness, love, prosperity, and wisdom is equally effective in establishing those states as our daily reality.

Vacillating when deciding whether or not to trust ourselves with the freedom to make a choice reveals our devotion to avoiding genuine choice. It is also one of our more proficient ways of encouraging the mind to continue its internal struggle. We have each inflamed the mind's internal war through our endless application of—yes, no, right, wrong, stay, go. Repeatedly, we trap ourselves within these internal tug-o-wars by incessantly second-guessing our every thought, action, and ability. What a clever means of avoiding choice altogether.

Empowering ourselves with the liberty to issue Free Will Choice is an invitation to all our inner levels to set down the habit of struggle. To gently conclude struggle—all struggle—stop tip-toeing around the periphery of life by engaging in the quest to heal, release or extinguish everything labeled as personal imperfection. This begins with *noticing* the distance we have already traveled and the vast personal presence we have reawakened by way of that journey. A large percentage of the wounding experienced earlier in life has been soothed through the spiritual, emotional, and psychological understandings since developed. We have funneled much time, energy, and focus into this research and the results are now internally evident, even if not completely acknowledged.

Being so thoroughly immersed in the on-going quest for inner restoration, is what caused us to consistently overlook the degree to which it has already transpired. And still, we proceed onward ever-seeking that elusive moment in which we will magically recognize it has occurred, that we are whole and—finally—enough. Due to the renewal that has already taken place the predominant number of self-judgments we yet carry—the negativities we express—are merely habit.

It is time to renounce our fondness for provoking internal conflict. Relax this overworked practice of self-repression. Love yourself enough to no longer batter yourself—from the inside out. Activating Free Will Choice is an energizing step in this direction.

One of the most potent reasons for our fear of making a choice is we have allowed ourselves so little practice in freely doing so. Subject to the strength of our self-devaluations, the muscle of Free Will has been left to sit in idleness. It has become weak, atrophied. Now, enjoy exercising these muscles by walking forward in the autonomy offered through the ever-present promise that every being in this universe is endowed with Free Will Choice.

This means no longer claiming to want something, some experience, some new expression of life while either wondering why these events have not been surrendered into our days or developing a self-brutalizing chart for manufacturing achievement and acquisition. Wondering and driving the self are both aspects of the victim game, self-demoralizing amusements in which we are highly accomplished.

We are Humanity. We are Awareness. We are Divinity. We are Consciousness. We are the universe in expression of itself. Freeing our choice to become manifest is a most uplifting means of developing intimacy with all of this inner strength. As we practice Free Will Choice, just as we practiced walking in our earliest days, we establish authentic relationship with the greater body of our awareness—our consciousness. There is no greater enhancement to our experiences, no more fulfilling means through which to have a positive impact within our own lives or the lives of others.

Actuating choice is a gentle movement, not a challenge to prove that we can. A need for proof or a need to know if we might succeed is a fast-track into struggle. Instead, the use of Free Will Choice is the smooth and patient motion of being present with ourselves, listening to our intuitive levels, hearing and feeling the messages of our senses and responding on that vast body of input. Feel the flow of any choice as it moves through your body and rises into your consciousness. Proceed from this space of enhanced awareness—take a choice based action.

Having followed the steps let go. Showing up for yourself in this honest way is all there is to do. In fact, to continue trying to do anything exhibits a lack of belief that solely making a choice, stirring by gentle action, was sufficient. What comes next in supporting your choice into manifestation, will present itself to your consciousness in its own effortless timing.

In every instance in which we toy with internal questioning, tension is activated throughout our body. It is a habit in which we have long trained our muscles and organs. This timeworn tradition is rooted in our fear of making a decision that will produce an undesired outcome. This internal pressure is a significant hindrance to fulfillment of our Free Will Choice, a promise our mental commitment to inadequacy will be validated. Relaxing into whatever choice we make releases the physical, emotional, sensory tension.

Trust your choice will become complete. Remember, if the outcome does not prove to be what you desired, you still have Free Will. You can simply choose to choose again. So breathe, remain calm and allow the path you have selected to support your continuation. Through this ease, you will realize the actualized result of any choice, and reap the benefits of its effects in your life.

Genuine choice is based in calm, centered action—not words. It is the act of **being life**, a progression that resonates with the total endorsement of every level of our beings in interactive collaboration.

Our mind has had no access to clear choice because it could not make a choice; it could only offer a wide range of opinions which resulted in polarized confusion. We knew the visceral repercussions of this pattern each time we turned to it, and it alone, for a decision, advice or analytical assessment. Never did our dear mind offer just one conclusion; never was it composed, assured or peaceful. By giving ourselves the genuine freedom to play in the vast realms of choice, we cease to bludgeon our minds into perpetual self-doubt and the torture of the tired and long-played tug-o-war.

As we decompress, our mind settles into its authentic role. It was intended as a doorway through which all our levels can communicate with each other, our internal meeting point for collaboration between each of our essential aspects of Beingness. As all input marries into a single flow of wisdom the electromagnetic pulse of the mind directs it into the days of our physical lives. Our minds are also the electrical firing mechanisms that trigger emotional responses. Those of our faithful, wise, loving, and uplifting, selves, as well as the reactions created by our thoughts of fear, hesitancy, question, and anger. Further, our mind is the source of reason. It has allowed us to access many understandings that have resulted in forward growth for all of us on the planet. What it was never equipped to do was make choice independent of all the other, vital levels of our beings. At this point in our evolutions, remembering how to hear the messages sent by these levels, as a single viscerally experienced voice, promises to be an enlivening adventure.

How many times have you felt the exhilaration of true and pure *knowing* flow in a direction or decision, just to see that excitement wan over the next hours or days? This rush of energy is the result of having received unpolluted guidance from all of your senses and levels of internal awareness. As this multi-level input moved gently through your being, it spontaneously connected with a mental imprint of fear. This was projected around the potential movement. Immediately, your enthusiasm was quelled until the situation could be more *mindfully* inspected.

This is particularly true in instances when you did not take ready action. Moving on counsel delivered from all your levels—when speaking simultaneously—is an empowering demonstration of self-assurance. Acting places your choice in the *now*. Through the energetic infusion of your centered action the choice begins to reveal its newly created living presence.

If the manifesting energies are left to float through the maze of your mind, they become dispersed, connecting to all the "what ifs" of your imagination: But what if this happens, or what if that does not occur? Only by remaining fully present in the *now* and using your mind—rather than being used by it—does any choice have the opportunity to become physically realized.

From our current position of easing into invigorated self-revelation and presentation, we are in the most potent position for acting on our choices that we have known in this lifetime. However, fear of choosing is a long practiced habit, so remember to breathe. Breathe into your whole self. Breathe into your body through which the greater perception is moving, and breathe into your mind, thus oxygenating it and offering relaxation. Breathe into your physical senses so they may continue to offer viscerally experienced understanding. Breathe into the choice. Then act, while continuing to breathe consciously.

Accessing and utilizing our choice is not just a privilege, it is a responsibility. Free Will Choice is a great universal generosity given—without reservation—to each of us. This means that to override another's Free Will is to inflict fear and self-doubt, thereby usurping their inner stability. In the same vein, to actively move to overrule our own choice with question, distrust, control, or non-action is to undermine our own balance and centeredness. It is a responsibility to our whole selves to act on and from all that we are. Likewise, it is a responsibility to the planet and all our brothers and sisters that we utilize this gift of Free Will Choice.

It is through us, our actions, and our participation with our own life force that the miraculous within each of us is given clear and fluid access to the physical realm. Being the universe manifest into physicality means being the vessels through which the universal whole is able to bring more of itself into discernable presence, and this happens only with our open, lively participation.

Over time, we have awakened to greater understanding. This personal expansion has advanced us, individually and collectively, beyond many limitations. True, there are still undeniable examples of judgment, separation, and fear in this world, but much less than we would have witnessed even one hundred years ago. With each generation we have expanded our awareness and increased our demonstration of inclusiveness, first internally, thus externally.

Now, we are *noticing* that we have toyed with the current levels of non-trust for long enough and are prepared for yet another great leap in our unfolding self-awareness. Taking this step is as simple and gentle as **being as we are**, all that we are, in this moment. Witnessing the expanse of our internal unification allows us to cease pretending to be wounded or limited. Subsequently we free ourselves to play in responsible use of our power of choice, a fundamental access point to supporting our growing completeness.

Utilizing Free Will Choice also reminds us that we no longer need distance from all that is Divine within us. Nor is there anything gained in continuing to endorse structure's stories of our being *merely* human. Employing Free Will Choice is, therefore, the action of a spiritually mature individual and an effective antidote to all structure. Within active choice flows expansive opportunity for joyful living.

It is probable that when practicing freedom within choice—as a means to reviving self-trust—we will occasionally produce a less than desirable outcome. These moments will afford us the opportunity to remember that a less desirable result is not a condemnation that we, ourselves, are undesirable. Maintaining this evolved perspective offers the encouragement to proceed in choosing to choose again. Equally enlivening is remembering that we have already survived many such experiences. We can now add to our body of wisdom the recognition that it was not in spite of those challenges that we continued on. Rather it was because of them and all that we learned of ourselves in negotiating their journeys that our sense of Self is continuing to flourish. Instead of falling into the temptation of thinking our progressive movements have been in spite of choices judged as poor, we can further exercise our choice by opting to view the way many served as wonderful landmarks, subsequently catapulting us into greatly expanded self-comfort.

So instead of resisting life by limiting ourselves and inhibiting our Free Will, we are sincerely ready to choose boldly and freely. Sample how much fun life can be and how liberated we can become. Choose. Just like the waxing and waning of the moon, the ebb and flow of the tide, the energy of the universe is always in movement. These natural revolutions offer a brilliant out-picturing of the way our individual energy lives in a continuous state of giving and receiving. So if the choice you make does not prove to be a grand adventure, choose to choose again.

Enthusiastically assuming our responsibility of choice reminds us that we are not in any way slaves to our life, our spiritual path, or our destiny. We each have choice in every moment and situation. So in any area, in which enslavement rears its head, accept that your decision to avoid living a whole-self responsibility is how personal freedom has continued to elude you. Emancipation exists in knowing and owning this one inexhaustible truth.

Never would our inner wisdom guide us to select a life, a direction, or a destiny without assurance the journey would be infused with opportunities for ease and ecstasy. It is only when we hold our being hostage to negative self-imagery that contentedness, satisfaction or self-appreciation appear to relentlessly evade us. And it is only an appearance, instituted through habitual patterning. What is sincerely honest is that we are successfully avoiding their generous invitation to relax and Be.

Breathe. Release all anxiety by very simply ceasing to evoke it through question and doubt. Open your clenched fists and let go of the mental commitment to rehashing the ideas of what you want, but do not have. As long as you focus on what is missing in your life, you are directing those very experiences and opportunities to continue to elude you. Energy follows thought. It is scientifically substantiated that when we change our thoughts, we change the molecular structure of the energy within us and throughout the surrounding six feet of the space. Therein, attention to what one imagines them self to lack is a negative prayer for that scarcity to persist. And the molecular structure of the energy both within and around you will support that choice in sustaining itself.

By the same rule of science, accepting and celebrating your choice alters the foundational basis of the energy both within and around you, thereby creating a positive molecular magnetic through which your choice does blossom into your life. This exemplifies how it is that matching your frequency to what you desire grants it as your undeniable reality. Thus, in any area in which you are less than fulfilled, change your mind, make a choice. The molecular structure of your energy will naturally recalibrate to a frequency harmonious with that to which you have shifted your attention, and the choice will become fulfilled.

Additionally, as long as any of us implement words such as "I don't know, I don't care, I'll do whatever I'm supposed to do—whatever the universe, my higher self or God calls me to do," we are still hiding. These are phrases we fall back on to avoid accessing the manifestation of our choice while outwardly projecting responsibility for our life's circumstances. This is one of the more commonly practiced ways we become a spectator to life, rather than *being life*.

Moreover, as long as we hide behind words such as "I don't know, I don't care, I'll do whatever I'm supposed to do—what the Universe or my higher self or my destiny calls me to do," we are actively disempowering ourselves. Hiding behind words such as these—and make no mistake, this is hiding—is a means of holding ourselves in fear of life, illustrated through our unwillingness to play in the arena of activated choice.

As long as you hide behind words that promise any level of powerlessness, or imply that you are subject to another's authority—especially the universe, your higher self, karma or God, none of whom would never choose to direct you or take your choice from you—you are failing to stimulate life. You are acting as an onlooker, rather than a participant with life in movement.

We are each Free Will in action, Free Choice in motion; we are life force unending. Life wants to express itself as a festival of exhilarating experience. Be the exhilaration of each moment, and by activating choice to be just that, life shifts quickly and in unimaginably generous directions.

Follow the gentle path. Walk the course of Free Will as an impassioned presence of both your Humanness and Beingness in collaborative oneness. Express the happiness that is your innate nature. *Be life* by being transparently all that you are, just as you are.

Acknowledging Truth

We have each spent our lives in search of truth, both personal and universal. We study, pursue, and quest in our attempts to discover what the actuality of truth is. To a great extent, we have now come to understand that truth is individual in its presentation. The realization that we each have a personal truth is a common languaging and has the potential to serve as a great deterrent to judgment. Yet the quantity of judgment in which we still engage would indicate a lack of overall acceptance of this principle. The dilemma is that what we call truth is frequently little more than a thought, something of the mind. As we all possess differing mental viewpoints of virtually everything within our world, truth becomes little more than an imagined validation of our personal judgments. Only as we accept truth as a visceral experience and free it to move through our cells as a provider of expanded understanding, will we grasp any broad clarity around what is true of, in and about ourselves, our world, and our greater reality.

Relaxing into a full body comprehension that truth is interconnected with our individual freedom to choose is immeasurably clarifying. This sovereignty is life itself. The way the ever-evolving frequency of life continually feeds and regenerates us is a beautiful illustration of this reality. That is to say, and more importantly to understand, the universe—as a whole body of life-giving presence—expresses nothing but truth.

We are the children of the universe, created of the essence of universal love and generosity. That being so, the reality we collectively create while moving through our many experiences is the manifestation of how truth—authenticity of beingness—is physically witnessed.

A great deal is said about authenticity of self and all too often it is a term summoned for the purpose of judging another by citing their lack of that very state. It is also common to wield this term—authenticity—as a means of continuing to hold the great mass of judgment-based energy we carry in disrespect of ourselves. What is true is that if we are the universe's representation of itself as demonstrated through physical form, then all we are, do, and experience is authentic; everything in which we engage, is authentic.

Granted, it may be an authentic presentation of our internally warring minds in one moment, an illusion of our unhealed emotions in another instance, and a clear presence of inner wisdom in yet a different exchange. Nonetheless, all of these are representations of authenticity from some level of our beings—authenticity of our troubled state of mind as we fail to recognize the illusions within which we have held it captive, authenticity of how unprepared we are to feel our disquieting emotions, or authenticity of the peace and exhilaration that is our essence. All are the same, in how they each express an aspect of entirety of who we are. Whether it is a belief in our illusions or an absolute universal truth, each is an authentic conviction of what we envision to be our reality.

Within this cognizance of all that truth is exists the invitation to stop waiting for life to come to us, to deliver unto us, to bless us, and therein, make us more. What possible *more* could we desire to be— we are life—the very essence of the truth of this world.

Life—the embodiment of truth—dissolves the story, therein provides complete restoration to our emotional body. It severs the anchor of the personality and the wound, offering gentle encouragement for our mind to relinquish the habit of expressing itself as tormented with fear and to play in its growing vitality. It completely dismantles the asserted identity, which has always characterized our commitment to the illusion of separation and restricted our mind's ease while dampening its happiness.

That is the established purpose of these structures—the personality, the wound, and the asserted identity—to offer protection from seeing truth, from hearing truth, and from being truth. These are the tools created by, presence of and resistance to feeling, our long-waged inner turmoil.

In our confused state, we believed that we must accomplish a climb to perfection. We imagined our mind solely responsible for the entirety of who we are and expected no assistance from any other source. Thereby, we blinded our self to the truth that loving assistance was ever-available. The inability to notice this secured the belief in our innate wrongness. We feared relaxing and receiving care, convinced that instead we would be met with admonishment for our myriad of shortcomings. From this structure induced perspective, we were unable to recognize that these were all judgments, formed within our mind, and issued upon our whole selves. Within the maze of these illusions we were unable to comprehend that each was a diversion to what is—and has always been—true.

Releasing adherence to structure allows us to gently rest into a broad understanding of truth. To fathom the expansive accuracy of this, let's begin with the realization that there is no "the" in truth. Truth is—not static, absolute, or staid. It is neither an object, or definable by a simple recitation of facts and data. Rather truth is a living presence, and the very electro-magnetic continuum that sustains each of us. It is the basis of our unending expansion. Subsequently, we fear truth for it is our authentic face; and due to our self-judgment we have each gone to great lengths to deny looking upon this reflection with any complete candor.

Consider the diverse illusions we have each created to avoid witnessing what is true of our beings. Remember all the striving and studying we have pursued in search of that seemingly illusive treasure—happiness. The overwhelming majority of this has focused our attention outside of ourselves, distracting us from the vision of our ever-present inner truth.

Yes we do meditate, practice yoga and engage in any other number of rituals for the purpose of peacefully settling within our own skin. But having felt the silence or heard the quiet, gentle voice of our inner wisdom, we have immediately looked outside ourselves for signs of the correctness of what we received, validations of what is true. These symbols are imagined to be found in rainbows, animal messages, repetitions of three, or any other random occurrences to which we have assigned unreasonable importance. It is true that the universe and other beings with which we share this planet speak to us through a plethora of avenues. However, it is equally true that incessantly seeking and analyzing these messages to infinity is nothing more than a means of sustaining our external focus. Through this, we are able to suppress the still quiet voice within that is ever speaking to us of all the truths we have actively sought to disregard lest they contradict our judgments, limiting beliefs or self-criticisms.

Witnessing ourselves and life as profound illustrations of truth—perpetually shifting and changing expressions of an ever-expanding reality—we connect with our own infinite presence, the innate core of who we are. From this point of uniting with ourselves from the inside—out, we naturally claim the responsibility of confidently living our most honest truths.

Because truth is not linear or static it cannot be fully unveiled through the mind. This is an essential truth. It is an outpouring of life expanding presence, an understanding of personal awareness, and can only be known through experience. Each of the physical levels are vital contributors to incorporating the fullest spectrum of what truth is, offers, and has to share. Through the messages of our body—visceral messages, sensory messages—our inner wisdom communicates to us as an audible voice of truth. It emits its awareness with great clarity—through wellness, through aches, through illness, through ecstasy.

Shunning these many emotional body and sensory expressed truths was never the mind's overt goal. Having been so long forced to comply with structure, it simply lacked the ability to recognize them as *being* truth.

Although truth is not structured it is consistent. It is the circumstances that manifest truth filled revelations into our lives that vary, just as our actions do from one situation to another. It is this unpredictability, combined with the mind's fixation on precise deciphering and defining that present the greatest challenges and sustain our inability to recognize truth, even when deliberately revealed. This is additional motivation to relax into the body and feel the reverberation of clarity emanating through your cells.

As we rest into unwavering, intimate relationship with our body and its messages, the natural result is a clear rapport with truth. To discover this, there are several absolute universal truths we can follow as guides.

Truth: *We are each where we have chosen to be.*

So often we hear someone, or ourselves, speak of where they "hope" to soon be, or of how they "can hardly wait" for this moment or that experience. Frequently, we overhear a conversation of how one's plans and visions were upended by another person or situation, or of how they cannot understand why the universe, karma, or God has left them feeling so lonely or unsupported. Within each of these circumstances, the truth remains the same. We are always *exactly* where we have chosen to be and we have always chosen to be *exactly* where we are.

Granted, we may not have chosen this exact happening in a single, clear and specific moment. Yet, if we reflect honestly on our past choices and consult our inner levels of profound wisdom, we will begin to *notice* how our patterns created our current circumstance. Through this clarity, the lessons that we are now—and may have repeatedly—offered ourselves become apparently understandable. We stop playing victim and our path of forward movement is instantaneously smoothed.

Truth: *We are all doing exactly what we have chosen to do.*

Upon realizing we are unhappy in our jobs, unfulfilled in our relationships, or lack thereof, or dissatisfied in our living environment, again, there is only one place to look: within our own choices.

This can prove challenging. We expend a great deal of energy avoiding *noticing* ourselves with complete candor. A great tell-tale signal of intentionally self-directed blindness is when we hear our own words or thoughts proclaiming, "I already know this," while witnessing ourselves proceeding in worn-out patterns that have repeatedly delivered unhappy consequences.

If we are, in fact, doing exactly what we have chosen to do and lack fulfillment, this is a wonderful time to activate our ever-present Free Will Choice and choose to choose again.

Truth: *We are, in all moments, experiencing exactly what we have chosen to experience.*

There are uncountable ways to choose the experiences of our lives. A majority of these appear to exist beyond the reach of conscious selection. This is another of our many fantasies. All of our experiences are chosen, and by us. On those occasions when you are tempted to play powerless victim bear in mind, that this is a Free Will universe.

Our confusion around what we did to enact a choice for those undesirable moments or experiences often arises when we discover ourselves affected by the delayed reaction time of the universe. We make a choice in October of one year, and the resulting fulfillment does not show its face until March of the following year. In the ensuing period, we have moved forward, set aside the choice and resulting immediate experiences generated during that earlier time. Therefore, when the longer-term effects enter our reality, we rarely think so far back as to trace the line of trajectory that brought about our current circumstance.

A notable contributor to numerous delays is the time it took us to let go of the energy so it could become manifest. As we clench our fists in an attempt to hold on to any desire, we ensure it will remain merely that. Setting it down, becoming fully engaged in the *now* of our lives is the only way any energy is free to manifest as a physical creation.

Whether or not we choose to become still enough to connect the long ago choice with the current events, the truth will not change. We experience absolutely nothing except what was chosen by our own actions and reactions. All too often our experiences are blamed on the universe, or the others who share our lives. "What do I have to do to receive what I desire or believe I deserve?"

Begin by at least considering that this is a loving, nurturing universal reality that created and continues to sustain us. In our absence of self-trust, and trust in all-that-is, we are the ones littering our lives with occurrences that leave us questioning and lonely. The greatest desire of the universe is to shower us, continually, with all we could imagine and more. All we are asked is to listen for the voice of our inner wisdom, hear the truth it is eager to share, and follow the guidance being offered—from the inside-out. Additionally, it is valuable to remember that when we do not follow our inner guidance and subsequently find ourselves in an undesirable situation, it is in no way an expression of universal punishment for having been incompliant. It is simply that we opted-out on taking the path of least resistance that was beckoning us. The unpleasantness we are experiencing is the result of our own choice for the rockier path.

Truth: *Life is our mirror of what we feel and believe **of ourselves**.*

Is it fun being you? Are you happy? Do you wake from your sleep each morning excited to see what the day will offer? Are your hours showered with miracles? Do you go to bed at night with a heart overflowing in thankfulness for the multitude of surprises that lavished your day? Do you have a body of community, friends, and family with whom you are in flowing, mutually supportive relationship? Do you *live* the understanding that every human on this planet is your brother, your sister and open your arms to each of them fully, without hesitancy, scrutiny or judgment? Are you fulfilled? Truly fulfilled?

If the answer to any of these questions is less than a clear, rich "yes," a valuable follow-up is: "Why do I not love and trust myself enough to have and experience _____?"

The authority to change any "no" to an abounding "yes" rests completely in your own hands, or more accurately, your heart and your choice. You are aware of what you feel lacking. Now, acknowledge why you are not ready to support yourself by receiving and experiencing. Know that if you do lack, you are holding a self-judgment in this area. Conceding this single point—without analyzing it and yourself to bits—begins to dissolve the unwillingness and un-readiness long secured by self-judgment.

The universe is the embodiment of love and support. It would never withhold from one of its beloveds. Only we, ourselves, would treat our hearts, lives and each other with such abounding disregard and find so many ingenious ways with which to do so—all supported by expansive justifications for our actions. Embrace yourself boldly in all areas of self-inflicted lack. You have the potential to shift any space of less to an absolute experience of overflow—instantaneously—by choosing to choose again.

A great truth of this world that we have repeatedly denied is that life is simple. Subsequently, truth is also simple. If you are not experiencing simplicity, you are likely engaged in the old tradition of persistent struggle. Simplicity presents richness of life, richness of experience, richness of existence. There is no lack within simplicity, as lack is the very thing that causes complication, which results in struggle. Each and every expression of lack is based in an elaborate belief system constructed by the mind, born of its own experience of daily struggle within its confused self. As our mind returns to peace, each of the old beliefs created while in its earlier, more polarized state will spontaneously dissolve.

Unwillingness to be ease-filled in any area of our life is the actualization of a choice to experience struggle as an inescapable reality. Just as the mental tug-o-wars were not inescapable, neither is the gentle continuation of ease and happiness unattainable. If we are living in struggle, we are not living truth. Truth begins with ease, with acknowledging that happiness is innate to our beings, and in generously sharing this state so others may witness its ever-present availability. Through this active choice of mirroring, we reveal truth to ourselves.

Experiencing truth and living its ease of self-embrace does require readiness. We speak of our willingness to do something. At times, we hear ourselves virtually pleading with the universe, our higher selves or the Gods of Karma to respond to our willingness. Now take the next progressive step. Willingness is a passive action. It is a valuable stride on the path to readiness, but still contains a lingering desire for someone or something else to take the lead, to show the way.

Readiness is active. It holds no hesitancy, or desire for external rescue. Readiness embodies the power of knowing, the knowing of our beings as lovable and gracious, the knowing that Free Will is unwavering, the knowing that we are an expression of human vibrancy. It is through the passageway of readiness that we are free to activate our choices, release struggle, and live as the quintessence of truth.

The ability to see, to be, and to know truth is all based on the level of commitment to being alone. So become alone. Not lonely—a state based on the perceptions of the personality and asserted identity. Being alone is the progression beyond the limitation of all structure. To be wholly present within yourself is to be alone. Becoming "wholly" yourself is to become *unafraid* to be "only" yourself.

We are the embodiment of all that is loving, generous, peaceful, and celebratory in this universe. Each and every one of us is the physical living presence of all that exists, has ever existed, and will ever exist. Whatever your preferred language, at an ultimate level we were each created of the great "all that is" of this universe. As such, we are in every manner the physical representations of that same infinite presence. Even in the way our bodies and energetic systems continue to regenerate themselves through all of hardships we have self-induced.

Enacting a state of becoming alone allows us to feel safe in letting all the ideas of who we are float away. As we release all the definitions created over the years, we awaken as the enlivened human representation of the universal state of all that is.

Becoming alone activates an internal wholeness of presence that sustains us in being unafraid to sit still with our mind silent, to let just the rumblings of our emotions be the only voice we hear, and to rest in the peace that they are not going to betray us. We will be ever lonely—a state created by the attempts to silence our inner emotions—until we are happy in our aloneness.

One great prevailing truth is that we have each spent many moments, days, and years in the space of "lonely" while mistaking it for being alone. We have reached out to others, clinging to them in impotent attempts to abate the emptiness that echoed as a great and torturous isolation. A majority of our intimate relationships were established out of a longing to connect with another as a way to feel, what we then referenced as, complete. All we succeeded in providing ourselves was a reduced—conscious—connection to our inner loneliness. Until that sedative wore off. Then the knowledge of our prevailing loneliness rose up in a great roar. All too often *fault* for this entire emotional spectrum was projected onto the formerly beloved one.

Through most of these attempts to diffuse our loneliness, it was our mind that provided our only company in this self-imposed state of individuation. It was the mind that helped us to feel less alone. In many levels of our beings, we fully believed that the mind was our only sincere ally, the single presence we could really count on to be present for us. This is why in our most fragile times, it was our mind to whom we turned first.

Repeatedly, we sat with our minds as they churned, agonized, and dissected the moments and experiences of life. Many a scenario was dreamed up by our mind for our entertainment, even when the experience would have seemed anything but entertaining. Our minds were the friends who created stories of success in the aftermath of pain or betrayal. They stood between us and our emotional bodies, thinking through the possibilities of what the emotional flow might be saying so we would not have to *feel* the messages. They aided us in protecting ourselves from the discomfort of an onslaught of sensation that we believed ourselves unprepared to navigate. It was our minds that created visions of great victory in moments of penetrating loneliness and bitter despair.

Now it is time to move beyond the loneliness that will be ever present as long as we believe our minds to be our dearest—and only true—friends. In becoming alone, we re-establish the connection with our heart, our senses and this is the doorway to realizing a state of comfortable self-intimacy. This is the internal space through which we realize that *we* are truly the greatest friend we could ever desire.

Additionally, to release ourselves from the restrictions offered by the personality's definition, to move into greater depth of embracing our whole selves, trust yourself to become no one.

This means releasing all isolation imagined within oneness to reveal the vast truth of our infinite connectedness. Further, through the conscious realization of our inter-connectedness, our mind can release its notions of separation and fully embrace a state of oneness within itself, which inspires wholeness that unifies all of our multiple-levels.

A compelling passageway into our deepest inner selves is the doorway of emotion. Consequently, rather than reacting to your feelings by fleeing into the safety of your mind's chatter, invite those emotional currents to tell you the truth about what they are communicating. The reason our emotions have been so frightening is that we have allowed our mind—even implored our mind—to interpret them. The definitions the mind assigned the expressions our emotions offered were a means of avoiding resting into the depth of hearing, feeling and absorbing the truth of the messages. Now let your sensations share what they know, rather than attempting to think through them. Only in allowing them freedom to flow, and feeling—not thinking, but feeling—their movement will we know ourselves—truthfully.

We have each experienced sadness, betrayal, and a plethora of other less comfortable impressions. However, most generally when these arise in such intensity as to be unavoidable, our mind is still hard at work. Per our request, it has defined them for us, spoken of the unfairness of having this delivered to us, and assessed courses of responsive action. Further, our mind has engaged in harsh judgment of either ourselves, the other who served as a catalyst to the pain, or both. None of this has led us to full comprehension of the personal expanse available in remaining present with these emotionally charged opportunities of self-revelation.

Sit with your feelings, with your mind silent; therein, you will arrive at an organic insight to all you are being shown. Rather than imploring your mind to define your emotive state, the cause and the reactions that should follow, allow a true knowing—which is based in a resonance that moves through your body and all your senses—to deliver a full disclosure of understanding. Through the path provided, you will discover a new level of being present with and as your complete self, combined with the satisfaction of having traveled a full cycle of learning. This is the entrance point that leads us into the unbridled expanse available by becoming alone.

At the same time, become insignificant. Become one single cell in the entire united body of existence. No longer cling to the illusion of solitary individuation that can provide only feelings of loneliness and seclusion. Expanding beyond the misdirected ideas of secularized insignificance, our minds and bodies are free to release all the disorder these belief systems created. These distractions were designed to avoid connecting with the sincere flow of our emotions. In no longer running and hiding from the messages of our emotional bodies, we afford ourselves the opportunity to comprehend that our fear of them was founded in mere fantasy.

As we become still and hear with our entire being, we place ourselves in the position of becoming familiar with the voice of our inner wisdom. Thus, we reclaim full recognition of our connectedness to all that is.

Additionally, as we relinquish our need for self-importance, and become only one of the stitches in the quilt that is the entirety of Humanity, we remember what occurs when a single stitch is dropped. *The entire thing begins to unravel.* Recalling the importance of each individual stitch, we see anew the innate importance of everyone who is here on the planet. Thus we are liberated from the idea of being individuated and isolated while simultaneously reawakened to our true universal importance through the interconnectedness of all that is.

Becoming alone, by seeing through the illusion of individuation, re-connects us to so much more of ourselves that we can no longer fit into the small definition that words once offered. This seemingly small step advances us beyond the labels we have attached to ourselves, so we can become intimately familiar with our authentic internal fabric. Therein, we begin responding to life from the entirety of our truth.

This is the time of truly coming to know oneself. Not the created identities, but the self. Not the multi-levels of "I" based in our lineage, but the authentic self, the expanse, the presence of Beingness.

In entering into communion with who it is that lives beyond the definitions and ideas, allow yourself everyday to have absolutely no pre-conceived idea of who you are, or how you are going to respond to any moment in life. Reply to nothing without first becoming fully present in the *now*. Allow what is offered to flow into you, into the depths of your heart. What does your core have to say? Listening this deeply, this clearly, is the exploration of how far out of your comfort zone you are willing to tread in order to ascend beyond the grasp of mental restriction and definition.

This empowers you in each moment of every day to adventure into varied opportunities with more self-honesty than previously known. And with each new step, you further dissolve the habits of old to awaken into the entirety of your presence and empowered Human Beingness.

Beyond Repression

ow do I express the greatest love and trust of myself?

How do I express the greatest love and trust of myself? Use this question as a guide rail. Pose the question, but expect no direct response. Let the inquiry run over and again, as an endless loop of tape in the back of your mind. Periodically, pull it to the surface of your consciousness and be present with it. As you feel it, speak it out. Allow the frequency of the question to flow over and through every cell of your body.

Do not turn to your mind for an answer, which is not to say that it will abstain from offering many. The mind has been serving us for all the days of our lives. One of its primary means of attempting this has been by responding—abundantly—to each curiosity we consider. Through our many journeys with the mind we have each learned to ignore the input, and it is this ability we can exercise in these instances. Supporting our mind in its on-going journey to flow undisturbed, without engagement, it discovers the ease of settling into collaboration with our greater awareness.

With the submission of this question of love and trust, allow life itself to be the response. Presenting this same question repeatedly—with no anticipation of an intellectual reply, no participation with the input that our mind will surely offer—life itself begins to shift. As a new rhythm establishes its inner harmony, greater numbers of synchronistic occurrences present themselves into the fabric of our days. This is the response from which we will receive the most profound benefit—the responses of life speaking through living expression.

As the momentum of the words and their intent become an established pattern, circumstances and opportunities begin to come together in ways that could never have been guessed. Life settles into a smoothness of flow beyond anything we could have written or drawn for ourselves.

As this occurs celebrate—yourself. Acknowledging what you have accomplished in relaxing sufficiently, as to allow this new flow, adds great momentum to what has begun and it expands into a regular pulse. By continuing to pose this straightforward question—to yourself—and rejoicing all that is revealing itself, you express a sincere self-trust that the steps you are taking are the answer. As this becomes your natural rhythm, life is experienced in fullness. Structure is retired and true awareness becomes the norm.

How do I express the greatest love and trust of myself?

By letting life support you, guide you, and bestow upon you all of its wonders. This is exactly what occurs when you are *in life, being life*. Retiring the old traditions of studying life—pursuing the understanding of life, questing for the meaning of your spirit— spontaneously resolves all expressions of self-hindrance and self-repression.

Interacting with life directly is how you will come to know it and be in active receipt of its communications. This is *being life*. No longer playing spectator is the assurance that you will receive and sincerely experience the fullness of the body of life.

We have each sought to resolve the dilemmas of our constructed illusions by thinking through them, and have repeatedly found ourselves tangled in the maze of their multiplicity. As you now travel beyond the quest for answers, you are beginning to allow the expressions of peaceful resolution, to any potential question or wondering, to rise within your cells, into your awareness, into your relationships. Subsequently you are going to witness your life, your mind, and relationships flourish and become the enriching blessings they have always held the potential to express. This is the enlivenment available from having retired as the director of your life.

To express the greatest love and trust of yourself, be spirit—activated through a physical body. Be Humanity. Do not analyze life or your human self, be that living presence, for that is our indisputable truth. By activating rather than defining, we each express the wholeness we have sought to understand. In the dissolution of all control, competition and comparison life itself is free to celebrate you with bountiful gifts.

In the absence of these old toys we each reveal a graceful expression of our innate passion, we live our inner truth. By being in attendance *as* life, playing as ever more fluid expressions of life being itself, we communicate passion through our every word and action. Thus life is expressed as the fulfillment of passionate *beingness*.

Being the animated illustration of passion-filled life invites larger and more significant expressions of sweetness into our days, and they begin to present themselves in a manner that further inspires our celebration of life. From this perspective, we are the recipients of our most penetrating internal wisdom. Propelling ourselves beyond all habit of repression is the action of living truth as an experience of transparent aliveness. This collaboration with life carries an invitation to relinquish resolution of the mind; relinquish resolution based in definition and identification rooted in structure. Embracing authentic resolution is understanding life as its own passionate inspiration.

How do I express the greatest love and trust of myself?

By consistently posing this question to the deepest levels of your inner self, any fear formerly presented into the fabric of life has nothing left to cling to and simply fades away. Each day becomes an exciting adventure of further awakening to who you are, combined with an expanded knowingness of your internal greatness.

With your innate magnificence becoming the accepted manifestation of life in every passing moment of every passing day, your awakening assumes its natural stride. You pump gas into your vehicle and a new awareness of yourself rises to the surface. Suddenly, unexpectedly, you are enlightened. While selecting groceries at the market, enlightenment settles as you see yourself clearly for the very first time. Enlightenment is not a mystical state achieved only through quiet contemplation or sacred ceremony. It is a *natural* state of being with and present as your complete self.

This is our age of coming into *being* our boldest and fullest selves in all the expressions available within each day. As our awareness rises to replace the old mind games of self-repression, instances of further expansion into an enlightened state occur in easy succession. This establishes a provocative personal connection to our vastness. Enlightenment upon enlightenment. By continuously and merely ceasing to play in the old self-repression games, we are liberated to flow in free self-expression and we remember our complete aliveness. All genuine components of life exist in the continuation, while having no potential destination. Therefore, our most sincere reason for life is to continue for the pure joy of the adventure, not for a potential reward at the end of the ride.

Moving beyond words, beyond dialogue, beyond definition is the path to becoming. This is the grand adventure through which you will *notice*, retrospectively, that each resistance previously held has begun drifting into memory. Long held habits that did not honor your being no longer fit and fall away with virtually no effort. These were the conflicts that trapped and befuddled our dear mind, which is now progressing into its own re-blossoming stillness.

As this organic evolution accelerates, wider and more expansive spaces begin to place themselves in the center of your life, between the moments in which your mind replays the well-established habit of speaking to you in unkind, unsupportive ways. This quickening in our evolution waters and fertilizes the expanding sensations of happiness, freedom, and utter contentment. These are moments to *notice* and honor. Just as focusing on our deficiencies enhanced them, *noticing* and celebrating our progressions will expand them with that same dependable momentum.

This shift in focus to all that we are and the growing happiness of our days will produce a cessation of all inner drive to hold ourselves in reflexive alert. Our body begins to ease into a more natural position. One appendage, one organ, one muscle group, one nerve group at a time surrenders the act of continuously standing guard. The punishing rigidity in which we have held our body is a prime contributor to limiting the amount of life's energy we are able to express. Each time our body becomes taut, it ceases to allow life's presence to flow. As medical science has now established when we tense our organs and cells become starved for life-giving oxygen. Optimum health, mental clarity, sensory aliveness and emotional freedom are reduced. As the energy feeding our physical levels is reduced, our body shifts into survival reactions, which activates our primal fear and places the mind on hyper-alert. In those moments the activated participation of our true awareness is hushed.

As we are now releasing the commitment to a specific and verifiable destination, and replacing it with a clear focus on continuation, relaxation is expanding throughout the multi-levels of our body, mind, and emotions. We are completing our expedition into self-abasement, self-abuse, and withholding from ourselves and becoming completely immersed in the love and reverence of who we are, have always been, and have now come to recognize as the truth of *self.*

How do I express the greatest love and trust of myself?

Breathe, exhale fully, feel your body relax; hear your mind settle into the silence. This is the natural result of no longer holding yourself in repression. Breathing in this way while fully embracing your inner silence allows your mind to realize that everything is fine. From its own exhaustion, it will welcome the opportunity for this respite.

Our minds are weary. During the long journey as a wounded self, they have worked far beyond their capacity. With the resurrection of our inner wisdom and our conscious movement into living unreservedly, we are now each eager to gift our mind a much deserved rest.

To encourage this while supporting our minds in the transition from confusion to ease, become worshipful of yourself. Not the ego's old duality-based adoration that was founded in a level of idolatry, but a sincere and profound honoring of the splendor of you—honoring of you as inherent wisdom, as a living, sharing expression of Human Beingness. For that is our most authentic reality. We are birthed of the love of this universe. Therein, we are the full expression of that love; we are, quite literally, that love in walking, talking human expression. Acknowledge yourself and all on the planet as enthusiastic advocates of this unending love, given the gift of physical life. This is a most profound step in expressing resurrected self-love and self-trust.

How do I express the greatest love and trust of myself?

By not seeking to know the answer to this question. By being, in a gentle and natural pattern that invites the very love and trust—of which the question speaks—to be our source of nurturing. As we live this reality we also rest into alignment with our passion, wisdom and vitality to experience ourselves as innate completeness.

Express the ultimate level of love and trust of yourself by not seeking any longer, by only being—by being wise, clear, impassioned life.

Allow this question to be the journey. No more figuring out, just knowing through living. The next great journey we are each ready to embark upon exists beyond the definitions that our mind can create. It is the journey of uninhibited living.

Whole Self Communication

As with all things, communication, true conscious communication, begins within. To our detriment, this is the very level of communication of which we have been most afraid. Thus, offering further endorsement to our questions of self-trust. Each time we ignore our sensory and emotional dialog distrust is enhanced and the expanded self-questioning further silences the cellular conversation. The two actions exist as mutually repressive traditions.

Over time, we have each developed an overwhelming number of tactics for suppressing our internal voices and the self-trust they have the ability to resurrect. To this end, we have raised the volume of our world to a veritable roar. Louder cars. Noisier, busier music. Increased volume in theaters. Many of the commercial advertisers on television have realized our heightened and finely honed ability to tune out the world in which we live. Subsequently, increasing the volume on their advertisements to such a point that it is often necessary to mute the commercials in order to remain comfortably in the room.

As with all things of the physical realm, the intensity of these outer sounds is a clear indication of the inner bombardment to which we subject ourselves on a continual basis. Since one of our mind's primary roles is to catalog information for future access, it is busier than ever keeping pace with everything we attempt to crowd into any given day. Therein, it is a key contributor to the ever-increasing internal noise. Subsequently, we ignore most of the messages offered by our physical body and walk through life in a state of sensory numbness.

There is an old and valid teaching: All we need to know we carry within ourselves. At our deepest core, we are unlimited wisdom and from this place nothing is hidden. Yet there is much more spoken within this ancient sentence than simply the reference to our authentic nature.

Our bodies carry messages and understandings that are insightful, profound, and ever available. Unfortunately, they also remain mostly unacknowledged because we have forgotten how to listen for them. On the occasion that we do hear the voice of our body, due to lack of practice at this level of inner communication, we do not understand the meaning or significance.

We were each gifted five physical senses. Sight. Scent. Taste. Touch. Hearing. We are taught from childhood to listen with our ears, our hearing sense. However, this is only one approach to listening. As we connect attentively with our sense of touch, we are able to hear what our body is telling us of its experience. We learn what offers it pleasure or discomfort. Therein, we develop a clear visceral understanding of our states of ease or discord. Our sense of scent is the strongest and most impactful of all our senses. Listening within to what it has to say invites us into far broader comprehension of how our physical world is influencing us at any given moment, and how that is affecting our overall state of mind and emotion. Hearing the messages of our sense of taste connects us to both our bodies and our lives in a way that expands our awareness of each from an intricately subtle level. As with touch, scent, and taste, we can hear what we are seeing through the way our bodies respond to what our eyes are showing us.

As we listen for our body's responses and reactions to sensory input, we expand our access points for connecting with our emotions. Through the electromagnetic waves that move and stir our physical body, we gain a broader understanding of the effect of any exchange or situation. Therein rests the message, or teaching being offered through that moment of life.

By listening to our whole being, we become fully equipped to respond in a manner most gentle and uplifting to ourselves and all the others with whom we interact. This is our most profound expression of communication, and a valuable approach to establishing intimacy with and through our entire being.

All too often, what we do instead is block the subtle and continuous messages of our human senses. This is the very reason our world has become so loud. It is our attempt to gain our own attention. Conversely, this is why we often find ourselves in retreat from the world at large. Feeling simultaneously inundated from within and without, while attempting to suppress both, is simply exhausting.

As with the increased sound of our world, the voice of life has had to increase its volume and exaggerate its approach to secure our attention. As we proceed through our days, ignoring the gentle messages meant to alert us, we experience uncomfortable occurrences. These were often easily avoidable had we paid heed to the soft, quiet voice within. On other occasions, these minor annoyances are the voice of life reaching out to get our attention. When allowed, life will use the gentle waves of sensory input to redirect us from a path that is leading to potential upheaval.

We now understand that each experience of our physical existence is our own creation. We are additionally aware that this is not necessarily from a conscious space. Choosing to reject or ignore the voices of our physical senses is one of the more effective ways through which we actively choose any number of the upsetting events in our lives. Opting to tune out our internal alert signals can also be a choice for an unpleasant outcome.

What if it was not just more annoying static from our physical world that we were ignoring, but our gentle intuitive voice? We see the results of this in many instances when an accident occurs. Maybe a coffee cup is knocked off of a counter. As the cup sails toward its ultimate destruction, we realize, one instant too late, that we had known this was getting ready to occur.

These instances regularly present themselves. Yet because we are so acclimated to discounting any potential value in the noise emanating from our minds and outer world that we commonly override the gentle, quiet voice of our senses, emotional bodies and wise intuit. Thus we are unable to hear ourselves being guided toward soothing experiences.

In any case, reviewing the internal messages that passed prior to the event will most often reveal the precise second during which we chose the direction that resulted in the undesired outcome.

In truth, we experience far fewer surprises in life, which are of an unpleasant nature, than what we have tried to believe. Many signals are delivered in advance of each defining moment that left us feeling life had deserted us, or failed to offer rescue from a particularly unraveling circumstance. The reality is our internal voices were speaking all along—life was signaling—and we were numbly paying no attention. Possibly, we believe that we were alert, but the event still occurred. In these moments, it is more likely our focus was placed singularly on our mind's goals, which traditionally supersedes our cellular, sensory, and intuitive inputs.

We have each spent many years and decades with our mind's influence stifling the voice of our cells, organs, and our internal wisdom. From this act of control, commonly misinterpreted as self-protection, it eliminated all internal communication with every level except itself.

The busyness of our lives is a prime motivator in not slowing down enough to connect with the physical senses. This misdirection of attention is pivotal in the eruption of illness, both minor and severe. The body is inherently self-regenerating and maintains a constant awareness of its own functions. By connecting with all of our senses, ceasing to dance around in our mind, or be overpowered by the external noise of this world, we can know well in advance exactly what the body wants. Fulfilling these desires, we enhance and sustain a gentle life experience.

This level of internal communication places us in cooperation with the whole of our physical form, allowing us the insight to serve it as fully as it has long served us. Being consciousness connected to physical forms, we can come to think of our bodies as tools or vehicles. Consequently, we offer them only the maintenance we view as convenient. When we activate as full expressions of our entire presence, we become collaborators with our physical forms. We offer kindness to the body that allows every level of it fulfillment within the physical experience. So rather than dictating to our body, being critical of its presentation and continuously driving it beyond all reasonable limits, become its bonded partner. Listen to the voices of your body, and as you do, all the areas of life can express themselves more fluidly in a way that becomes a life-giving element of consciousness.

In respect to the other approach of communication, that which is focused externally, our great internal wisdom is more effectively expressed through the act of listening than speaking. Again, it is your body through which this application of communication is centered. When engaged in communication with another, you can determine if you are focused in your mind or settled within your body by listening to your physical senses. Do you feel the way your body is responding to the energy of the words the other is saying? What is the energy they are sharing, and how is it affecting your skin as it touches you? What are your eyes seeing and relaying to you through this exchange?

When we commit to this level of listening, of receiving, and of presence with another, we possess the ability to be of true valuable assistance. By being totally present and listening with our full self, awakening within our senses and hearing with our body, we become most influential expressions of supportiveness.

All the gyrations that have been attempted and the mechanisms that have been accessed, all the talking and thinking, and thinking and thinking are nothing more than communication with and through our limited self—communication with and through our mind. Incessant mental activity is often a continuing endeavor to work to establish value outside of ourselves. Frequently motivated by a desire to validate our capacity to be of assistance, possibly even of service. This is most commonly demonstrated in the ways we respond to our friends, family, and associates. We struggle to present all the most correct answers and most insightful understandings. In reality, the words we speak and thoughts we offer may be of great value, but possibly only to ourselves. In screening or evaluating what another person is saying through our well-honed filters, the observations of our mind are often all we absorb. Even in our mind's current state of beginning to rest this remains true, but now it is based solely in habit. Practicing and becoming fluent in whole-self communication is now easier than ever before, due to the degree of peace the mind has already adopted.

In assuming a stance of increasing internal silence, sitting in complete transparency and enjoying our inner serenity, not only are we able to be of authentic service to another, but also to ourselves. Through our transparently tranquil presence, we finally allow ourselves to see, to know that we are entirely enough just as we are. By doing nothing but showing up, attentively, compassionately, we become the embodiment of whole and valuable service that is the reality we have sought and pursued.

One approach to practicing this depth of communication is relinquishing the habit of reaching out to offer solutions to another. Be still within, calm your mind, and just hear them. Relax your mental processes and hear them fully. From this position, what you ultimately present as a response that speaks to the entirety of who they are, rather than being little more than your mind's acknowledgement of their mind. Formerly, rather than offering service or solace the established tradition resulted in your ego initiating a battle with theirs.

This deeper approach to communication has become all but a lost art in our world—listening from one's fully transparent self—and then speaking to the whole person before us. An unfortunate reality of our collective lives is that there have been very few moments in which any of us have felt truly heard, and felt that what we had to offer was so valuable as to draw another's complete attention. Now we are ready to regenerate this tremendous gift and thus, remind each other of our unlimited value.

For the most part, we as humans are only able to listen to the extent that what we hear does not challenge our own belief systems. To use our freedom of choice to opt to listen is a significant move in breaking the habits established by our mind, therein providing it expanding states of restfulness. To choose to hear beyond the roar of our mind's resistance and to remain transparent in the moment, first, tells us that we are not at the mercy of our mind's conflicted confusion—a point with which many of us are yet struggling. Secondly, it signals that whatever is being mirrored—whatever is causing our outdated mental beliefs to feel challenged—is something from which we will no longer strive to hide. This sends a compelling message throughout all our internal levels that we are ready to embrace each hidden part of ourselves, to take an active stance in loving all of who we are.

Think of the times in your life when you felt you were really heard. Did this not enrich your moment, enhance your day, and expand your sense of well-being? Knowing that we are important enough to be worthy of being heard is a powerfully uplifting validation. When you listen to another fully, the most miraculous thing is that they are able to hear themselves. For when we are heard, we are able to be entirely present with ourselves, rather than engaging in old habits of wrestling for space.

Another common expression of the mundane level of communication is presented through the need to speak what we believe to be our intuitive inputs. Frequently these messages are given without the recipient having asked for our insight, or without our first inquiring if what we want to share is welcome. In these instances, even if it is a genuine and clear intuitive perspective, offering that information without request or permission dishonors the person to whom we are speaking, for the sole purpose of glorifying our own minds and egos.

As illustrated through the law of critical mass, if every one of us on the planet would make a full commitment to listening, to whole communication, through transparent presence with every other person with whom we come in contact for only one day—and if all of us did this on the same day—the entire planet would become the sanctuary of sincere inside-out unity, that we have each been seeking. We are fundamentally incapable of attentively listening to another— offering them the occasion of feeling sincerely honored—without gifting the same to our own beings. Communication through full-body presence is the creation of absolute perfection of flow, both within and without.

Transparently authentic communication is expressed when all the cells of our beings are allowed to be present within any exchange. When the cells of our body are given license to play in lively interaction, simultaneously, our inner wisdom is completely freed to participate. Living in a state of authentic communication allows the frequency of compassion to channel through our bodies and reach out to all who surround us. Through this our inner wisdom communicates to every individual we encounter, inviting them to rise out of seclusion and play in the exhilaration life expresses when allowed to flow unimpeded.

Our body is our primary means of maintaining communication between our multi-levels of awareness and all that is within the greater world. As we have come to understand, the mind has spent much of our lives expressing its most intensely frightened state. With it now returning to peacefulness, this is the time—the appeal—to return fully to the body, to hearing the communications of all of our senses as they flow throughout.

Practice sitting, perfectly still, in absolute internal silence—no mental chatter. Breathe. Be. As your mind becomes serene, initially the silence can feel deafening. Remain within it. Allow yourself, for possibly the first time in ages, to become aware of the depths of your being. Hear your body as it moves and shifts within itself. Let it speak in its physical tones. Hear the voice of your breath, the combined messages of your physical senses.

Within this space, this moment, exists tremendous curative presence. As we connect with our natural internal balance, the gentle peace—the activated flow of our awareness—becomes liberated to move through our cells and enrich our entire being. Without the mind's voice rambling on, issuing its many dictates, telling our body how and where to *seek* life's blessings, our internal wisdom and vitality are stimulated and our depth of personal comfort is infinitely expanded. In the absence of all searching for them, our blessings are received spontaneously.

Remain within the silence, and you will learn to recognize the voice of your heart. Through this voice, you hear all life is saying through you, for the heart is the connection point to your inner wisdom, your passion, and the access point to all that is. This is an intoxicating antidote to the dance of confusion, control, and chaos. It is an expression of self-acceptance that naturally leads to retiring the old habits established by the once conflicted mind.

Do you trust yourself to hear what is really being spoken by your cells, your senses, your organs, your skin, and your heart? Do you trust your own life-presence? If not, how will you trust yourself to hear your power? And what is this often mentioned thing called personal power? It is quite simply the voice of your senses and heart in flowing collaboration with your internal wisdom, strength and vibrancy. Again, we are called back to our bodies.

A great deal of our unwillingness to hear internally, to listen to the messages moving through our physical forms is centered in our lack of trust *for* our bodies. As acknowledged, it is an infrequent occurrence for us to look in the mirror just to praise our physical forms. We judge, criticize, decide we need to lose weight or have cosmetic surgery, but we do not love our bodies. Further, we do not trust ourselves overall or the continuation of flow of our own wisdom and vitality within our bodies. To remember how to hear the messages of our bodies—a skill not exercised since we were very young—we must re-embrace our lost expressions of trust. To live our genuine radiance, embracing trust of our physical, emotional, sensual, and mental bodies is essential. Distancing from any of these physically oriented expressions denies us the fullest life possible.

Each time we speak the words "I hope," we are communicating to our cells, our senses, and our subtle levels, "I do not yet trust myself." Each time we feel the need to repeat or reaffirm a choice, we are communicating to our cells, our senses, and our subtle levels, "I do not yet trust myself." Each time we question our choices or actions in any way, we are communicating to our cells, our senses, and our subtle levels, "I do not yet trust myself." Each time an action is taken followed by pondering if we were right, wrong, appropriate or inappropriate, we are communicating to our cells, our senses, and our subtle levels, "I do not yet trust myself."

Our mind, once deeply conflicted, at war within itself, has not yet set down *all* the long-held fear. This is the struggle, and a long practiced means of internal communication that was ever-self-defeating. Significant ease has settled within our mind, and is yet continuing to expand. To support this growing peace continue to play in listening to every level of your being. This is a most gentle path to establishing consistent internal communication.

Take any action and continue into all the moments that follow, confidently. Thereby, communicating self-trust and acceptance throughout your body. Practicing this trust communicates to all your internal levels a strengthened awareness of your value as a human on this planet. This becomes the new standard of inner communication as you walk through the days of your life.

Gratitude and Humility

I n all sincere discussions of gratitude, it is also important to review humility. This is an expression hugely misunderstood in our world. The majority sees humility as meekness, sacrifice, service that extends outward only, and never inward. Additionally, humility is often confused with actions or words chosen to minimize ourselves or minimize the actions we have taken.

More often than not, the word humility is used when we are attempting to convince ourselves and others that this is our motivation, while we are clearly expressing little to no humility whatsoever. On other occasions, it is mutated from its clearest essence into a self-effacing, self-minimizing exercise or description. In actuality, humility is a deeply heartfelt, overwhelming love that flows into every cell and space, excluding no one and no thing.

Authentic demonstrations of humility exude clear and bold self-awareness—ever-expanding consciousness. As this is articulated through physical, mental, and emotional action, our inner wisdom is given air to breathe. In its cleanest and most genuine presentation, humility is living—the act of truly *being life*. Coinciding with our mind's expanding peace, we realize that no amount of wandering through our imagination will create the most fulfilling life available. This allows us to appreciate that living our deeper inner potential comes only as our innate wisdom weaves with the grounded wholeness of our human presence.

By giving our wisdom the liberty to express itself, we open to receive, accept, believe, and know, without searching and reaching. Thus, we eliminate all physical and mental participation in control, competition, and chaos. This is the transition from structure-dominated living to playing in the completeness available through actualized humility.

Furthermore, the enlivened presence of humility rests in the constant action of gratitude, of knowing that life encompasses more than we can see, more than we can imagine, more than we can give away, and more than we can ever use—except through giving away. The expanse of humility is realized as one stops toying with self-restriction and receives all they could ever desire. Letting go of the reins, silencing the habit of mental dominance established during the decades of our mind's voice reigning supreme, supports us in becoming the physical realization of the abundant generosity of this universe. This is the face of humility in action.

Ease and abundance of life presence in movement is the very thing we have always desired, and have sought to create, yet until now it has remained an unfulfilled dream. Becoming the living presence of humility is experienced by centering ourselves into the heart of each new moment, and allowing our inner awareness to communicate through our human voice and actions. The resulting connection promises ease of creation of all the states of being toward which we have ever struggled.

Our undivided and multi-sensory focus into complete interaction with any occurrence in our days is also the action of expressing the humility that naturally re-awakens our lost trust. All non-trust exists outside the realms of humility. Absence of trust drives our actions, and illustrates a belief in knowing more than the entire universe in terms of what we deserve and what is being offered. Nesting into all expressions of receiving is an ultimate movement toward reestablishing this trust. It illustrates our willingness to see exactly what our inner wisdom desires to bring into this world and acknowledges our human self as the vehicle of physical manifestation. Through this movement of humility, we remember to trust that everything we are given will be loving and supportive. Further, through all we receive we are reminded that in simply maintaining an active relationship with our inner wisdom while remaining fully connected to all levels of our human self, anything we could ever desire is ours. This participation with humility is our repeated introduction to authentic gratitude.

At a core level, gratitude is the vehicle through which one moves out of overbearing mental input and into the living presence of trust. Gratitude is the action of shifting from "I need, I lack" to "I have, and am, and come, let's play. How happy is my life. How incredibly fun it is to be me."

These each appear statements of boldness which by societal interpretation is antithetical to humility. Again we witness a belief rooted in structure. It is through the bonding of boldness and humility into a single balanced presence that each supports the other into its own richest potential. It requires boldness to say, "I Am." Bold is the voice that speaks of love for all, when judgment is the standard in our world. But there is no lack of humility in this.

Speaking in gentle and pro-active tones for peace when there is so much encouragement to clamor in aggression is powerfully bold. Yet again, this represents no absence of humility.

Through boldness, we are compelled to love the one with the loudest voice of judgment, in spite of the fact that they clearly cannot yet love themselves. Most generously, within the humility expressed through this boldness is the invitation for the other to consider loving themselves.

Being the face of loving boldness as a vehicle for moving beyond false humility by ascending it into an authentic expression which weaves into gratitude and connects them both to trust of everything we are, on every level. For any of us to recognize how amazing we are, is a bold demonstration of trust so strong that it reaches through the fog of our long-held confusion.

Listening to life through the ears of our innate level of humility, we are able to feel the gentle voice of our inner wisdom when it reminds us, "You are a treasured and blessed one." In hearing this, *authentic* humility does not immediately seek proof, nor does it try to demonstrate the incorrectness of this message by withholding any blessing. Humility inspires us to spread our arms and say to all that is, "Yes," in recognition that the face of all knowing wisdom is a quantum—and bold—leap into personal wholeness.

Humility sustains us to trust and float beyond the well-entrenched beliefs of need and of less than that we have watered, fertilized, and cultivated for so many years, decades, and generations. Likewise, it is through humble trust that we have the insight to grasp the absolute wonder of ourselves. It is humility that compels us to trust ourselves with all the words, actions, and experiences communicated through our lives.

Until now, we have been too afraid, too untrusting of ourselves to allow these amazing personal revelations. Great boldness is also required for us to surrender the security and familiarity of the fears that have so long directed our self-image toward fragility. So too is great boldness necessary to jump into the deepest pools of self-allowance, self-acknowledgment, and unlimited gifting to ourselves in all areas and on all levels. Yet again, this boldness is the activated presence of humility.

We have sought, studied, and pursued in any variety of ways and directions for eons. It is valuable to realize the extent to which this quest has disassociated us from our humility. We believed that only through this quest would we happen upon, as if tripping over a rock, the presence of comforting wholeness we were repeatedly denying, repressing.

Now be the living illustration of trust by emulating humility in all your days; become present as the whole of who you are—Human presence empowered by Beingness. No longer withhold from yourself anything your happiness, strength, and wisdom, are eager to bestow upon you. Instead, be in an ever-flowing state of gratitude for all that you are, which is the position of remaining continuously open to receiving from every direction. Receiving openly and broadly reminds you of just how valued you are which stimulates the longed for resurrection of trust. This reemergence further aligns you with your natural abundance in every area of life. The authentic flow of giving and receiving is revived and finally, the deep sigh into peace. For surely there is no peace found in consciously disassociating from our inner wisdom and abundance which when free, bond with our human adventurousness. This is the very marriage from which emanates life's most joy-filled experiences. In fact, to disassociate from any level of this gift is the polarity of humility.

Humility infused with gratitude and freed to flow through each of our senses introduces us to a depth of enlivened feeling richer than we have ever known. Without our human form, how could we know what it feels like to be physically embraced, and yes, to even feel unwell? For an absence of wellness is nothing more than a signal from our body that we are not nurturing it sufficiently. As humility and gratitude awaken our emotional body, our senses are infused with the experience of being fully centered in our life. Through this enhanced connection, we discover eminently more potent sensations when falling in love, feeling rain on our faces, or enjoying the earthy scent of a forest. What a brilliant plan and clear path we have been provided for saturating ourselves in the potential wealth of being simply and amazingly human. Be in humble gratitude for this gift of physical life that continues to give back in every moment and exchange.

In reviewing society's perspectives around gratitude, it is most commonly thought to be a thanksgiving for what *was* received. But that is only one small aspect of its vastness. Gratitude is a living breathing expression, and much like ourselves, gratitude is so much bigger, so much grander, and so much more enriching than what meets the eye—particularly the limited eye created of our illusions.

It is not the relief experienced when the dreaded bad thing, or less desired result, did not come to pass. Ceasing to confuse gratitude with relief is vital to enlivening our days and enriching our interactions. Additionally, gratitude is not a goal-oriented search for something for which we might become thankful. Rather it is a joyful recognition for that *which is*—just as in the example of our authentic presence, which is already giving to us in each and every breath.

As an ongoing expression of *now*, authentic gratitude is the very energetic and emotion-based frequency that does enliven the minutes of life. As we remain balanced in our own center it continues to expand within all our physical levels. The more of life's blessings we are open to receive, the more of its own richness it is able to express upon us. This bounty comes as an enticement for feeling, tasting, touching and connecting with everything that moves through us. Therefore, it is gratitude that beseeches us to fully acknowledge—on all levels, in all ways, and through all expressions—that we fully deserve. Each time we refuse ourselves any blessing—through doubt, through question, through apprehension of an unknown outcome—we distance from both humility and gratitude. In acknowledging that our inner universe is infinitely wise and possesses a broad scope of understanding all that we deserve, combined with a love of gifting to us, humility and gratitude become actualized.

It is through exhilarated gratitude that we are able to express a joyful acknowledgement of all we are. This initiates our spontaneous re-birthing which results in a release of all states of self-denial, and harmonizes us into the realization of unrestrained acceptance. Through this shift of consciousness the universe is given limitless permission to shower our lives with unimagined goodness. Regardless of your personal name for it the great Love that is the source of all that is, desires to pour over us, into us, and through every corner of our existence. Gratitude opens the gate for Love to be able to offer the gift of itself to us freely. As we live the reality of authentic gratitude married to humility, there is no longer anything we are willing to withhold from ourselves. Trust is reawakens and we are free to *be life* in concert with all that is, through every adventure of our days.

This ignites an ultimate level of aliveness within our beings and our exchanges. From here, love, presence and Beingness flow through us and our lives completely unhampered for we are no longer holding any secret space within—there is nothing more we desire to keep hidden from ourselves. Retiring mental definition to this extent furthers the bonds of humility and gratitude, which unites all the levels of our mind, body and spirit more succinctly.

When you *notice* yourself indulging in thoughts of lack, you are actively avoiding oneness with the continuing flow of your inner strength and wisdom, which exist in an ever-faithful state of giving. Ideas of lack—in any area—block our ability to accept this nurturing. Moreover, playing with ideas of lack derails our resurrection of self-trust because lack exists outside the reality of both humility and gratitude. Therein, all commitment to lack dis-empowers us completely.

Acceptance of the natural wealth of our inner vitality allows it to demonstrate its greatest desire—to love us, in all ways of endowment. Living the limitless blessings of health, support, love, and financial freedom, shifts us into acknowledgment of that which we are—the authenticity of loving Human Beingness in its every manifestation. That is the actualized truth of who we are, not merely a destination we are seeking. Breathing into this truth, as expressed through gratitude and humility, we give ourselves permission to continually experience how thoroughly remarkable life is.

Many ongoing struggles are rooted in the belief in scarcity, a primary structure of thinking in our current world. This is why, up until now, the illusion of scarcity—be it modeled in our lives through friendship, finance, love, support, or health—has been key in sustaining our question of trust. Now at the edge of the great precipice of recollection of our innate prosperity in every arena of life, we are invited to access the vehicles that will lead us beyond the abyss of mental conflict. These being the expressions of humility bonded with gratitude, leading to the resurrection of trust, resulting in full empowerment of our lives, our days, and our every experience.

As a result our passionate core is able to guide our focus beyond our own daily experiences to include all that exists. The authenticated presence of humility expressed in union with gratitude encourages participation in life more expansive than we previously had the energy to consider. We are inspired to receive, share, accept, and pass on, knowing that we cannot share and pass on until we have first received fully and openly. Proceeding boldly forward, continuously expanding into more all-encompassing interactions our passion blesses not just us, but all with whom we interact. Opening our hearts to be in mutual exchange of gratitude with the each person we meet places us at the center balance point of giving and receiving. A visceral reminder of how all of us on this planet are, in a very real sense, brothers and sisters to one another. Thus further actualizing the vast loving potential, which is our authentic truth.

A powerful aide in cooperating with all we encounter in this mutual conversation of gratitude begins with remembering that the physical realm was created especially for us to share as a single body of Humanity. Truly, this has always been the most significant and apparent indication of our inherent affluence, but it has also been a hard-drawn realization for our mind. Our society, our structure, has denied this at every turn. Our collective history is filled with myths of our being placed here due to having been removed from grace, or as some other karmic hardship over which we had no influence. Now as the creators of our society and our structures, it is time to welcome the certainty of the gift that physical life was intended to be for each of us.

The wonder of this planet is a phenomenal illustration that we are the recipients of immeasurable and unquestionable devotion. As we express the heart of humility, bonded to gratitude and trust, the recognition of this certainty becomes the living essence of our daily understanding. Through these comprehensions, we are free to set down all resistance and take up the enthusiastic play of *being life.* It is this very adventure into which our inner brilliance has most looked forward to participating. This is our ultimate life purpose; to express the lighthearted discovery of being humans in love with all of Humanity.

Having considered a more richly authentic expression of humility expanding our understanding of its partner, gratitude, is equally assistive. A sincere comprehension of the frequency of gratitude presents the realization that its polarity is fear. Each time we find ourselves wandering within the confusing vortex of fear, we are ignoring the ever-available presence and soothing affects of authentic gratitude. Additionally, each time we run from fear we are actively suppressing our access to the comfort singularly available within gratitude.

In either case, whether finding ourselves surrounded by or hurriedly dashing to escape fear, the remedy is to stop, become still. Be the moment—not *in* the moment, but *be* the moment itself. To *be* the moment, implement the art of *noticing* from the perspective of *now*. Being with yourself in this honest, free way of gently *noticing* yourself, your whole self, exactly as you are here and *now*, is infinitely liberating to all levels of your being.

The predominant amount of fear still carried is founded in our dread of experiencing our own emotions. All avoidance to hearing our internal messages is the expressed suppression of humility triggering a disassociation from gratitude. As we rest into humility we become open to seeing ourselves clearly, honestly, to *noticing* whatever is. *Being* the moment allows us to express gratitude toward the messages delivered from our multiple levels, which soothes our energy and allows us to understand what our emotions are revealing. Gratitude is our expressed thankfulness for all we have *noticed*, of all that we are, experience, express, and exude.

Through the perceptions of activated gratitude and humility our inner wisdom is beckoning us to take a leap of tremendous faith. It is asking that we offer ourselves an expanded awareness of who we are, what a wonder we are, and what a miracle our life is. This evokes a fertile and spontaneous participation with gratitude. Not a "thank you, thank you," effusive version, but a deep residing worshipfulness of ourselves, a deep residing worshipfulness of life, and a deep residing worshipfulness of our participation in *being life*.

As we are inspired to celebrate our grandness, illusions of lack, illusions of less than, and illusions of need are easily *noticed*, and the pictures, the stories melt away. This is the natural result of having been replaced by sincere self-awareness, by a visceral recognition of all that we have come to understand as ourselves. Having scaled this mountain, having discovered the completeness of ourselves, there is even more of life available to marvel in and for which to express profound gratitude.

Settling into gratitude and expressing humility provides yet another powerful key to dissolving the final voices of fear. Gratitude is the act of leaving the illusions offered within the established patterns of the past and honoring what is—*now*. Thus, gratitude exists in the space beyond "what if" and "after this or that happens." Supportively humility is the powerful idiom that fuels the things, the moments, the experiences of life that we did not request, have not sought after, have not longed for, and yet are ready to embrace exuberantly.

This is yet another encouragement to breathe in the gift that life is offering, the surprise of life demonstrating its own presence, its generosity, its love of you and its love of surprising you. Therein, you not only receive the gifts of life, but actually become the gift as you respond in gratitude filled humility.

Gratitude is found in embracing the moments that speak to the heart in a true exhibition of love. The one single rose that blooms after season just to express its own beauty. The spectacular bird that lingers on the fence just to share its magnificence and its song. The laughter we share with a complete stranger that lightens the rest of our day. Gratitude is found in being present for these moments— alive within the center of these moments.

Offering authentic gratitude for ourselves and our essential participation in the world creates a state of comfort in our own skin, comfort within our emotions, and trust of our own human presence. From this new space of internal ease, we are emancipated to offer generously toward our self and all others. Positioned securely within ourselves, what others experience is the real person we are— unmasked—as a whole being, stable, serene, and centered. They witness us as Human Beingness.

We now understand the potentials within witnessing for each other, but what about the value of witnessing ourselves? This is the act of being truly present with ourselves, present within each of our moments, and present with all the messages of our senses and inner voice. Witnessing ourselves is activated *noticing*. By witnessing ourselves, we are able to remember, in each moment, that we are ever-expanding wholeness. As we flow with the always-deepening comfort in our own skin, we easily recognize the difference between moving from reaction versus gently offering a response. It also enhances our awareness in *noticing* the times we are sleep-walking through our days and reminds us to wake up and be fully alive *now*.

Celebrating the gifts of this life, by *noticing* the ease with which they flow to us from every imaginable and unimaginable direction is witnessing the limitless magnetic of our inner frequency as it connects with our external reality. Only when centered in our humility can we understand the expanse of such unlimited expressions as being accessible through physical experience.

From there, all we previously turned our eyes from to avoid personal recognition become the very visions in which we can revel, for which we experience overflowing gratitude. This is the gateway to moving forward in life with enthusiasm for all that it is mirroring to us of ourselves. Gratitude for every experience and humility of ever expanding self-recognition is the natural flow of who we are at an authentically transparent level.

This same witnessing—when exercised from both from within and without—dissolves any residual tendency toward judgment, turning it into nothing more than the memory of a child's game. That so, gratitude emerges to fill us with the wonder of looking upon the diversity of this world and realizing ourselves as participating members. Gratitude is the gift that adjusts our vision to recognize the amazing uniqueness of our own expression of life, and to feel the extraordinary textures of life as exuded by all of us in loving co-existence. Freedom exists in this space of appreciation and continuation. Ecstasy is found in witnessing the inspiring illumination life can adopt when free to express in all the ways of its own choosing.

Free life to be itself. Let the wind blow through you. *Being life* is allowing the energy, the frequency, of life to flow right through another to you, and through you to another. This is the exchange of life's presence; this is the Beingness life exhibits when free to follow its own natural current. Do not hold onto or cling to any energy that comes to you. It is just passing through to enliven you. It is not yours to keep and in letting it pass through—you will not find yourself depleted. This world, and all that is life upon it, exists in a state of constant movement, a continuing celebration of spontaneous regeneration.

Life itself has no ultimate destination. Neither do we. What is given to us is an endless flow of blessings meant to pass through, thereby enhancing our days, and making space for the next opportunity of expansion. Gratitude for what is, the humility to be boldly present in each moment of *now* dissolves all lingering desire to seek an ultimate outcome. They remind us that we are each portals in the continuum through which life flows and expresses its own infinite presence.

Exuding gratitude toward ourselves, it grows into actual love of ourselves. This ignites continually deeper compassion toward both ourselves and everyone else, inspiring a spontaneous eruption of expanded awareness of gratitude for all levels of existence.

Completing the activation of gratitude and humility includes the awareness of how compassion is their fundamental partner. Too often when we articulate what we imagine as compassion, what we are expressing is judgment. We use phrases like "Bless their hearts" or "Isn't it a pity." In reality, these expose our belief that the one of whom we speak is a victim. Maybe it is life itself that we judge for having brought them great hardships. On other occasions, we imagine them as having fallen prey to another's misdeeds or ill-intended words. In any case, these are not phrases we would apply to one who we see as a blessed and therefore limitless being.

Engaging in this old way of thinking sends messages to our own subtle levels that we might at sometime fall to a similar fate. Each time we presume another as victim, we reinforce our own mind's conceptualization of its prevailing vulnerability. We reinforce its illusion of being its own and only source of support.

On the other hand, as we begin expressing true compassion for any other, we concurrently alter all self-perception. As we recognize the truest nature of those around us we ingest this very message with regard to our own beings and lives.

Transparently authentic compassion is centered in expressing absolute love. In this, it is anchored to gratitude. As we look at the situation of another and see them as a fully empowered being presented with nothing more than a challenge that they are fully equipped to handle, we elevate them. From this honest perception, we can also extend gratitude to them for gifting us the opportunity to be reminded of our own limitlessness.

It is the link between gratitude and compassion that reveals our truest motivations. If we are expressing words of gratitude and can simultaneously feel compassion, we know we are connected to *sincere* gratitude. Likewise, as we offer compassion, while experiencing an active sensation of gratitude, the purity of our compassion is validated.

In the same fluid action of looking within to *notice* the connected space of these two expressions, we will realize a profound level of gratitude for ourselves. By communicating compassion-fueled gratitude, we naturally embrace all the actions we have taken throughout our lives, including those that formerly evoked harsh self-judgment. Through grateful compassion for ourselves, we understand the challenging moments of life as having been great teachers. Each occurrence or action of our past that is viewed clearly spontaneously re-centers us in the *now*.

Humility expressed through gratitude and linked to compassion are the sensations of opening one's heart to continually embrace more, farther, deeper, to see and to know the never-ending shifts and flows within this dance of life lived in and through one's own Human Beingness. This is the face of gratitude, the expression of humility, the presence of compassion, and the reality of you as life in flow with all that is.

Authentic Responsibility

Through living and being our authentic responsibility within this world and each individual moment of our lives we cease to pretend. As humans guided through life by the illusions we created within our mind, we have practiced and fine-tuned many acts of pretending. Even now we pretend. As we struggle with our thoughts and choices, we pretend that we still have mountains to scale in our healing and our seemingly endless quest for inner peace.

In pretending, we limit ourselves by restricting the energetic movement of life in an endless exhibition of ways. Pretending that there is solidity we see life as a strenuous expedition to cautiously navigate. We assign solidity status to our bodies and to disease, believing illness to be an inescapable inevitability of physical reality, challenging and often difficult—if not impossible—to heal. We view our professional pursuits as subject to the whims of the physical world, and imagine them to be the providers of all we identify as our needs. A most significant point of assigning solidity status is witnessed in the area of finance. We view money as solid and to heighten the challenge, we envision it as being ever elusive. These are all acts of pretending, each strongly supported by the prevailing messages of societal structure.

As we now realize there is broad scientific acceptance that everything in existence is set in and governed by frequency, electromagnetic current. The only thing that makes maintaining our bodies, our emotional health, our mental acuity, negotiating our career path, or establishing financial balance difficult is our *resistance* to resting into a frequency harmonious with the unlimited flow of life's natural pulse.

Our bodies are fluid, energy running through a primarily water-based component. As the energetic stream of our emotions, our thoughts, and our beliefs float through our physical forms, readjustment is easy. Think of what occurs when electrical current runs through any liquid element. The current of the liquid body is forever altered. The same is true of our physical forms. So as we adjust our thoughts and belief systems to encompass this understanding, living becomes a far more gentle matter.

As with everything in life, the area of career pursuits is also subject to electromagnetic principle. When we participate in fields of endeavor that fulfill us while operating from a knowingness that we are blessed and valued members of this world, the molecular structure of the energy flowing within and around us shifts accordingly and all identified needs are met. It is not our employer or our clients or patients who provide for us. We are each providers to one another as we exchange energy, with service moving in both directions. As we exercise our gifts and talents while understanding that this is stimulating our energetic movement, we recognize the law of universal frequency as our provider.

Finance or more specifically money is nothing more than another representation of life's frequency in movement. Consider the term currency. It is based in the root—current. All that exists is built upon electromagnetic current, frequency, energy. Therein, finance or money can be nothing more or less than another expression of this same reality, this same scientific principle. Our ancient symbol of infinity placed into actualized application.

Referencing the specific of finance, a primary difficulty we as humans have repeatedly encountered rests in our belief that this is something different, something *innately* limited. We are taught to view finance or money as something separate from all the other currents in our world. It is imperative to recognize that any belief in separateness reinforces all other ideas of separation as being possible.

Therein, when we hold the current of finance in restriction, we also hinder life's natural flow to bless us in other areas and expressions. Conversely, as we actively and boldly participate in life, we allow ourselves to be gently supported by the current of life in all areas, expressions, and moments.

To set down this long-exercised game of pretending all we need do is practice authentic responsibility. This is as uncomplicated as gratefully acknowledging each gift and blessing already present in our lives. Remaining excited about being continuously showered with unimaginable surprises positions us in the heart of gratitude and aligns us with the frequency of that blessing. This is one of the most exhilarating reasons we are in this life, to play in open-handed receiving and to have fun with all with which we are endowed.

The deepest level of each of us is wise and unlimited. Our self-created challenge is the belief that our inner wisdom is something more, something separate from what we generally call "me." Through this skewed perspective, we inflict separation between the many levels of what is our singular wholeness. Thus, we exacerbate the very states that suppress an ease of *being life*. Rising to our authentic responsibility requires nothing more than allowing our human selves and the presence of our inherent wisdom to play in concert as fully supportive partners.

Allowing interaction between our inner intelligence and human levels dissolves the separation we have pretended to struggle to dispel. When dispersed, we naturally unveil an experience of self-love. Love of ourselves settles us tenderly and completely into the supreme presence of our boundless human potential.

At its core, responsibility is the act of inviting all our internal energy forward to express itself. By no longer repressing our energetic wholeness with demands for qualification, identification of a specific destination, or a clear assurance of perfection, it is free to arouse fulfillment into our days. Whether experienced through the energy of wellness, financial balance or emotional satisfaction, it is the same. Visceral recognition of any internal imbalance relaxes our breath, organs, blood flow and energy. Thus whole self equilibrium is restored. It is only opposition to this level of self-acceptance that suspends us in discord. Similarly, if an internal energy is one of empowered creation releasing it to spiral forward allows it to express all that it would, therein, physically manifest as an on-going life blessing.

It is an unalterable law of physics that as thought is given space and oxygen to expand, it connects spontaneously with the life-giving frequency of creation. Feel within. *Notice* the seed of what you desire and breathe into that desirable vision. Now, set down all further thoughts of it and go about that which is presented into your day. As you do, your creation is oxygenated with life and set free of the limitations created when in hyper-vigilant monitoring. Most naturally, it becomes manifest as a physical reality. This instinctive and elegant action of becoming physical requires nothing of us, but the original choice made through our own Free Will empowered by the release of all control. The prevailing law of universal physics does all the rest in actualizing any new creation into being.

If any doubt of this organic cycle of planetary physics in action lingers, consider how many times you have poured energy into a dread just to see it spring forth, fully manifest into physical life. If unpleasant creation is this clear and dependable, joyful conception can be no less so.

There is no internal qualifying necessary to achieve this state. The attempt to do so focuses the mind on old stories of perceived insufficiency. Additionally, you are not benefitted by performing specific acts designed to produce a particular manifestation, in a precise way or presentation. This would also focus your mind on ideas of lack, which would fertilize belief in need. *Gently cease pretending to be restricted.* Remain conscious that creation is inborn within each of us, and can be witnessed from any direction—be it wellness, prosperity or any other experience. Accordingly, any unbalanced frequency, formed of old commitments to need, will spontaneously dissolve. Your organic state as a creator will be infused and become fully evident within you and your life.

Stepping into our finest deliverance of responsibility is a result of concluding our game of pretending to be limited. Authentic responsibility is activated by rising to the call of ourselves—our true selves, our inner wisdom and our human potential flowing in a single resonant harmony.

Another exciting result of awakening in our expression of authentic responsibility is connecting with the inner call, power, and reality of our destiny. An important realization around destiny is that it is not a hard and fast plan to which we are commanded to adhere. It is not, as we have often pretended, an assignment or diagram set forth by someone or thing greater than ourselves. Our destiny is the design we create for our lives by responding to the energetic pulse of our inner wisdom and human presence when expressing harmonious unity. Therein, destiny is the path most filled with potential enjoyment of life in the physical realm. Our destiny is satisfied in each of the days we walk this planet, honestly and responsibly by expressing bold humility. Thus, living our destiny is an enlivening antidote to pretending.

Just as it is true that our inner wisdom and human presence contribute to the continuing creation of destiny, ultimately, it is we—by application of Free Will Choice—who finalize each selection for every direction upon which we embark. This understanding activates acceptance of authentic responsibility which creates movement beyond the trap of pretending to be powerless, pretending to not know, pretending to be any manner of less than. Accepting that we design this life as we are living it is a definitive expression of responsibility, as it silences any justification for playing in victimhood.

Living from an expression of responsible creation is the shift into being everything we have learned in a flowing easy manner of life being its own fulfillment. Therein, each creation becomes its own gentle blessing, no longer something we must pretend to struggle to design. Through living authentic responsibility, we experience the learning, the lessons—freely and gently. We no longer work them, no longer toy with them, no longer practice them, rather embody the living truth of the astuteness received from each. Living our authentic responsibility is setting down all pretending to live the truth of all we are.

Life is fluid. To realize we are living our destiny is not to say that our lives are predestined or orchestrated by some higher being, outer source or karmic debt or patterning. A game of pretending now played for long enough. It is an acknowledgement our innate wisdom exhibits in setting a course of ever-fulfilling progression. Within this exists room for unlimited variables. As we continually acclimate to the autonomy of Free Will Choice we create our reality in each breath we take. Throughout life, whatever destinies we have chosen have always come into presence based on this universal model. Therefore, should we choose at any moment to re-focus to an alternate path from that already established, these new trajectories will be supported as fully as the ones from which we departed. So now it is time to stop pretending that we are subject to the actions or desires of any dominating force of any nature. We are life as it expresses itself through our participation with ourselves, while play with our Free Will Choice, in a constant adventure of creating ever-expansive life options.

From this state of awareness, no longer does *need* have a place in which to express its illusion. When wedded to our authentic responsibility through thought and action, searching is recognized for its fruitlessness, seen as a grand game of pretending. As collective souls expressing ourselves physically, we are now ready to conclude all pretending and to nestle into the demonstration of responsibility as expressed through being all that we are. In doing so, lack—of any nature—becomes nothing but the memory of a game played, mastered and now retired.

Walking our authentic responsibility, we become the breath of life in this world, oxygenating life into all that we do, all that we encounter, and all that we share—one with another. In return, as we venture beyond all pretending and live the most authentically free existence we are willing to experience, life oxygenates us, transforming our days, and all that we touch.

Living the essence of responsibility is also sharing with all our brothers and sisters on the planet that we are each our own salvation, and that we are here to mirror and to witness salvation in each other until we are each living the freedom of salvation's presence. Salvation is nothing more than the clear progression from pretending to live life—while struggling and restricting ourselves—to allowing life its own evolution. As the energy of the universe is freed to communicate sinuously, it is able to travel through every one of us, enriching and enlivening each new space it enters. This face of salvation is rooted in the readiness to *be life*, and to freely share life's presence with all we encounter.

This thing called salvation is not something we are waiting to have bestowed upon us from an outside source, any more than Beingness is something for which we must qualify. Salvation is the presence of life in continual, unrestricted flow. We have been pretending that we have to do some special thing, perform a precise ritual, speak a specific prayer, to receive this gift.

Who we are and who we recognize ourselves to be has been evolving since we came to this Earth. It is this on-going truth that carried us from our early states of awareness into all we are *now*. It is this same ever present spiral of life that has elevated our collective mental comprehension through all the generational changes we can look to history and review. So now, as we set down all pretending, each of these ideas of externally produced salvation can also be set aside.

This is why we are all here together. We live in this physical realm as a collective and together, through life's many adventures, we have been remembering the truth of our lives and ourselves. By traveling through the many dances of physical life as a collective of mind, heart and universal wisdom, we remember that as one of us lifts ourselves up, then so too are all the rest offered this doorway to personal revelation. Remembering the possibilities within acting from authentic responsibility uplifts everyone collectively. It supports us in living our fullest and most enriched life potentials.

Demonstrating our authentic responsibility as a level of our growing unity is also the act of taking the hand of love, the hand of wholeness, the hand of all that is and welcoming it into our lives, minds, and hearts. This is all there is, our most sincere reason for being here—this remembrance of individual completeness which enhances collective oneness. And yet, this is not an ending. In reality, it is only the beginning.

Too often, we have allowed the societal perspective that we must be ever working on ourselves to become the perfection driving principle in our lives. Now all of our cells are awakening to the realization that this is not our purpose. Thus, we are welcoming the inspiration to celebrate the joyfulness of our humanness. Having traveled beyond the ideas that had us struggling in numerous directions to qualify for some unknown and unachievable destination, we are beginning to breathe true freedom. Enjoy settling into your body, your heart, each of your physical senses. Gift yourself the open moments to *notice* all that you are and the happiness you are experiencing within this continuing realization. *Notice* the gentleness experienced when resting into deepening connection within your many levels of consciousness, emotional openness, and sensory acuity. Thus life in the physical realm will reflect your impassioned enthusiasm for playing as Human Beingness.

This is the entrance point to the deepest experiences of excitement that can only be known through humanness. Authentic responsibility is the act of embracing life with the full passion that rests within the core of each of us and being unafraid to feel, live and ride the waves of this great internal current. Therein, life is given space, oxygen and energy to exist, to thrive, and to enrich—abundantly.

Noticing Projection

As we now realize, authentic responsibility exists as a living demonstration in all the moments of our day that we are *being life*. Projection has been a commonly utilized means of avoiding this state. This is witnessed as we *notice* our self grinding through a day, deciding to participate only to the slightest degree by only showing up—physically—with no active emotional or sensory connection. We do this when we have pre-decided not to enjoy any occasion or experience. Through our years and decades of playing back and forth with intellectualized approaches to steering through life's experiences, we have become proficient at projecting our *idea* of the potential amount of satisfaction available through an upcoming—while not yet manifest—occurrence. Frequently, without letting ourselves move into or sense any small instance of authentic living, we project our idea of the amount of pleasure available in doing so. Through the well-honed practice of projection we frame, box in, limit, and structurize any greater outcome to the smallness of space set by our imagination and its suppositions.

Our collective wisdom is now calling to each of us, to every brother and sister on the planet. We are being beckoned to rise to our promise, to be all that we are. This voice of absolute clarity is speaking to all who know wisdom, passion, and exuberance to be the authentic truth of themselves, beseeching each of us to *be* the physically expressed mirrors of these emancipating expressions. Our collective wisdom is asking us to release all inner conflict by breathing into the unification of every level of our beings. By answering the call—stepping up as our boldest selves—we are invigorated by our inherent internal strength and experience deepening enlightenment in each step we take, each word we speak, and with each thing upon which we place our hand.

At any point in our lives, whatever our molecular vibration as we pass through our days, every place we set our foot, each thing or person we touch with our hand, we leave a memory of our presence. It is an energy echo of sorts, a reverberation that affects all who come after us. So as we expand our awareness by doing nothing more than realizing our ever-existing aliveness, happiness, and wisdom that resonance spirals as an accelerated frequency. This is all based in the same scientific understanding that allows us to know that changing our thoughts changes the molecular structure of everything within and surrounding us.

The same principle illustrates one of the many miraculous ways through which we are continuously reaching out touching and affecting one another. Each person on the planet carries within their cells the awareness of being an essential link in the electromagnetic spiral of the world. In each moment, we choose whether or not to exhibit that inner knowing through our daily actions.

We have expended much energy playing, and not in the lighthearted way that was intended. Each of us has played at being small. Much focus and energy has gone into playing with being powerless. Imitating victimhood and playing with need are games of pretending we have all entertained.

Now we are prepared to grow beyond these games, ready to bypass the creation of inner conflict, release all polarized thinking, and relax into unified expressions of internal completeness expressed externally. We are ready to play as our unified selves and to enjoy each experience of our lives to the fullest degree. The time of delving into the structure of doing is now past. In these new moments we will find ourselves comfortably resting into the depth of being awake as life frequency manifest through physicality.

Be the answer to the call of this inner voice that is speaking great wisdom. This isn't hard or an invitation to endeavor feverishly. Our ability to rise to this occasion is carried within our cells and energetic fabric. In this very moment, make the activated choice not to do, but to be. Be the activated response to the beckoning of our collective insight. Cease to play in all projections by remembering that their sole purpose is to maintain and substantiate every idea rooted within the staid limitations of structure.

Initiating this choice aligns your human voice with that of your inner wisdom. Thus you become the invitation to those who have not yet taken the leap of trusting themselves to step boldly forward—into their own skin and opportunities. Living as the unified presence of human self and inner wisdom serves as stimulus for others to breathe and relax into being fully present as and within themselves.

Release all remaining tension; exhale all residual anxiety of wondering what, how, when or where. Simply exhale into the state of I Am, I Am life in movement. Exhale and let the projections float away. Let the structure evaporate by no longer feeding it with your own life energy.

This is what we do when we adhere to its dictates by, administering self-restriction, chasing perfection or singularly conclusive destinations, by playing in judgment and projection, by repeatedly denying trust to ourselves. Consequently, letting it dissolve is as easy as no longer complying.

We are ready. After long preparation we are ready. For eons we have fought to break structure down to wrench free of the weight of its burden. So many times we have cried out for a rescuing agent to lift us from behind our self-erected walls, forgetting all the while they were our own creations—fueled by our own projections. Through the encouragement of our confused minds we projected onto life the need for *it* to shift, the need for *it* to let loose, the need for *it* to allow us to be free. Now, step into an honest recognition of life and the inherent freedom it is ever-offering. In so doing, welcome the opportunity to live enthusiastically. Then look around and you will *notice* that *you* have centered *yourself* in the all-powerful position of *being* the shift, the place of *being* the letting loose, the full recognition of *being* freedom in its fullest expression and demonstration.

Freedom from projection blossoms with the active noticing of where you have been exercising its restrictiveness. So, *notice* the way in which you project upon any other. This habit is perpetually substantiated through the addiction to judgment. Each time we adopt any level of judgment of another we are projecting onto them what we think we cannot bear to witness within ourselves. Through this old habit we separate from the most powerful allies we have—our mirrors—presented in human form.

When becoming aware of a sensation of discomfort while sharing space with another, do not project your discomfort onto them, do not blame the way they address life for your internal unrest. Acknowledge that they are mirroring you to yourself. If you did not carry similar frequencies within, you would be capable of recognizing their personal discomfort while feeling no measure of conflict within your own body or emotions. Your compassion would be evoked in witnessing a brother or sister so bound by their fears.

Breathe, exhale fully. More oxygenating. Cease to play in projection and you will come face to face with your own fears, of yourself. No longer secreted away behind the veil of projection, you are afforded the opportunity for self-honesty. Acknowledgment that any, and all *internal* discomfort is your own. It is within your skin, emotions and senses, is it not? Accept the levels of yourself long held in such distaste, and you will witness the complete dissolution of the projections that repeatedly vexed you. Releasing your projections— one after another—offers the manifestations of structure increasingly less power to distort your reality.

Remember, we have erected and supported both sides of every struggle—those we recognize as emanating from within, as well as those that we project upon the outer world. Exhale the last strands of each projection. Now do nothing more. Just exhale. No struggle, no doing, no reaching, no efforting, just exhale. Then sit back and relax. It is done.

Allow any anxiety that moves within your body at the anticipation of viewing yourself with this level of honesty and lucidity to pass through and thus, be released. There is nothing else to do. Relax, be still, and let yourself float into the wave of your most sincere truth.

We have each done, and done, and done. Now stop. Stand still. Sit still. Allow life to show you that you will not be dropped, you will not be betrayed, you will not be left behind. These are all ideas of projection, illustrations of our lack of trust. It is in the stillness that these finally dissolve, effortlessly.

This step which we have each worked so long to reach, this step that we have struggled so hard to avoid, is only difficult to the degree that we continue to project our strength, our wisdom, or responsibility for our lives or choices, outside of ourselves.

Fall back into yourself. Free fall into life. Open your arms and fall back into your skin, your deepest self as if you were dropping onto a feather bed or into a great pool of water. It is not that any of us have ever been in search of the elements of our wholeness, vitality or conscious awareness; it is only that we have been on the road to no longer denying them. Within that journey now dawns the realization that this is not a becoming; it is only the remembering.

We are each remembering that we are not structure, we are nether weak or less. Projection is an aspect of both. Sincere honesty with ourselves about our absolute grandness is the single healing balm that can *remember* us into a state of ease.

In releasing projection, embrace the full expression of authentic integrity. Integrity at an authentic level is an absolute resonance of inner certainty. It does not project any expression of responsibility, but sees and speaks only of the strength and wisdom of all. It does not play small or look outside itself for rescue. It embraces the gentle power of its truth. To operate from an authentic level of integrity is to relinquish all judgment and projection, and to acknowledge all your wisdom, and utilize—freely—your Free Will Choice to offer only love and support in all directions in every moment, including to your own dear self.

The End of All Journeys

D o not hurry. Do not make it a mission. Do not need to. Do not have to. No longer hide from yourself. Take it easy. Enjoy. Choose. These are the actions of giving your authentic strength and wisdom open-handed permission to activate themselves through fully expressed Human Beingness. Therefore, it is also the path to progressing into a luminous state of *being life*. Initiating the sincere truth of ourselves "by" *being life*, is nothing more than the gentle action of relaxing into the multi-sensory, multi-level expressions that we are and have always been.

Release all lingering thought that any course of study in which you once engaged held the power to make you more. Let your ideas of who you are and what these added to your essential being fall away, leaving in their wake only the wisdom that was gained. Allow this to flow as an integral expression emanating through, rather than an external, thereby extraneous, validation of you. Whether they be intellectual, emotional or philosophical interests, each of those endeavors has served you well. They were in fact, mighty contributors to who you are now. But looking upon past undertakings for evidence of self-value is of no true service.

Life activates life. Seeking, studying, processing, and practicing are tools we have all used based in the illusion that they would save us— from our lesser selves. In actuality, it was only the strength of our commitment that has proven itself true. Certainly these wanderings entertained, and now, as we *notice* the resilience of our quiet depth, we unveil a sincerely honest self-recognition. We were never dependant on these tools to become who we are. The truest purpose they served was revealing this to us, exposing us to us.

From the exact instant at which we entered physical life, we have been progressing toward remembrance of our expansive wisdom and supple strength. Energy is life and energy is constantly in motion. It is always growing on and within itself, so we too have been expanding—from the inside-out. At times, the momentum has accelerated to a dizzying stride. On other occasions, our fears hindered the pace to a barely discernable rotation. Nevertheless, the energy of our authentic being has continued to propel us through all of our experiences. It is true that there have been times when it appeared to stand still, but this is simply not possible. In the instances when it seemed so, it was merely that our minds were in such turmoil that we were blind and mute to any potential progress.

By comprehending that energy, life, and we as physical beings are in constant—organic—evolution we discover the most amazing universal truths. Life is a given. Expanded awareness is a given. Our destiny is a given. Our strength and wisdom are givens. We do not have to strive, wrestle, qualify or study; all of these are givens.

This is not to say that study is negative. It is the means through which we learn to language all we are experiencing, thereby, offering ourselves ever-increasing perceptiveness to our innate vitality and brilliance. Nevertheless, to continue believing we must devote our lives to endless pursuit of these quests is self-undermining. Each evokes the energy of efforting, a weighty hindrance to tranquility and happiness. They restrict the freedom of our energy, our aliveness, from expressing its instinctive enthusiasm.

Searching for anything demands of our mind that it perform and produce while simultaneously being accused of lacking something indefinable, yet essential. Through this abasing pattern, we have cowed ourselves into deep resistance, turned our lives over to the pressure of control and competition; thus, found ourselves repeatedly lagging behind where we mentally dictated we should have been.

Concluding the long and often arduous journey of both mental conflict and illusioned separation stimulates recognition of them as mutually supportive saboteurs. From both active and more subtly influential mental spaces we have complied with the structure-driven compulsion to overcome these deficiencies. Thus, we have repeatedly reinforced the unwavering belief that we were persistently flawed. To varying degrees, we are yet seeking the comfort of knowing that we have achieved a state of whole-self unification. This has us continually envisioning ourselves in the earlier stages of becoming.

As we persist in looking to the mirror to discern the changes that cannot be defined—but that our mind claims must be present if we have, in fact, achieved oneness—we do nothing more than perpetuate the drama. Through continuing our search for what our mind defines as perfection, the borders and boundaries indicating our arrival are constantly extended outward, projected into the future.

Traveling and re-traveling this path, we pay heed to our emotions only when attempting to disentangle from what we deplore. We focus energy on our body solely to cleanse it of what we judge as restrictive. And yet where is the celebration of all of these aspects of our self? In what ways do we offer them the freedom to be *in* the experience of life?

Finally, we are ready to relax. Actively breathe into a state of ease, feel life's inspiration flowing through your veins. As a result, all the studies in which you have engaged will express their fruit fluidly.

You are complete. Allow this truth to evolve into an understanding that effortlessly settles you into balance within your center. Live the invigorated expression of your inner awareness in full physical presentation *as* Human Beingness. Visceral realization of completeness is what sanctions it, thereby you, to move through life with graceful ease. Exhale into your multi-level silence with singular attention on the *now*. Revel in your boldness, your sufficiency, your unquestionably wise self.

When allowed and encouraged to spiral as their natural expressions, our inner wisdom and stability teach us all we would ever want to know, bless us in unlimited ways, and shower us with surprising opportunities. It is this that joins us with them into a unified field of oneness. Innate Beingness playing as empowered Humanness.

There is much said about our ultimate destination being an actualized unified field, but what is this? It is nothing more than us, just as we are, when expressing wholeness through the union of each of our levels—mental, emotional and sensual—bonded with our inner vitality and insight.

Life is the teacher we have been seeking, but it is also the one we have most virulently ignored. Instead of living, we have dedicated ourselves to preparing to be ready for life. Simply living the internal freedom of personal expression already available in each new moment of *now* reminds us that every time we reach outside ourselves, using external barometers to determine our level of oneness, we reinforce the tired illusion of separation. This ever-present internal freedom also evokes the remembrance that we can no more qualify for Beingness than an animal can qualify to be a dog or a cat. We simply are. Regardless of the degree to which we deny this, it can never be anything less than reality. By the same token, as long as we are in the physical world, our mind, emotions and sensory experiences will remain vital aspects of our completeness.

Having realized that qualifying to prove our worthiness no longer carries any fascination, we are well prepared to release all work and remember our authenticity as unified wholeness. This will broaden the dissolution of any lingering ideas of separation and we will be naturally drawn into exploration of our life's passions. Shifting our point of focus to our whole, impassioned self will free our dear mental center of its burdens, furthering the unification.

As physically manifest beings we are not perfect, and yet we lack any sincere imperfection. We are one hundred percent of all that we are, and in this we are ever-enough while always evolving into more of that same presence. Welcome the comprehension that you are more than you have ever imagined. Stepping forward to express the "more" that we are invigorates the life presence that supports our every breath, life movement and human expression.

Acceptance of ourselves is the new adventure into which life itself is inviting us to play. There is no process for this letting go; there is no technique to be memorized. Conscious readiness to stop toying with the idea of separation begins by looking into the mirror with unreserved boldness, not to verify or compare, just to see our reflection as it is. From this first daring gesture, lovingly accept every aspect of this one who is reflected and be in appreciation for the perfection that is revealed in exactly the way it is *now*, today, in this minute.

A most glorious reality of our beings is that we are our own destiny. We have held the idea of destiny out in front of us as a means of relentlessly driving ourselves forward. We fear that if we do not continue to push ourselves, we will simply stop, sit down, give up, cease to progress, and never become sufficient. We fear that if we do stop chasing, we will be settling, relinquishing ourselves to an ever-continuing state of being less.

Take a moment. Look at your life. Feel who you are. If indeed, you did stop—right now—what exactly is so wrong with who you are, and what you have created your life to be? Reflect on an earlier time. Feel all you have become since then. This is not to compare. Simply *notice*. Now, rest into the memory of a past occasion when you experienced great quantum movement. Do you feel the ease that you were expressing in that exact instant? In truth, it was never the pushing that propelled us forward, but the times of peace that we allowed to flow between the struggles. In this new and current vision of yourself, witness how you are the destiny manifest of all your earlier selves—older, wiser, and far more loving.

Live from the center of your days and hours. Accept that with each turning of the clock, rising and setting of the sun, you become a new expression of your destiny, as it continues to fulfill itself.

As we persist in chasing the ideas of what our destiny will look or feel like, we unconsciously fray our energy, de-unifying our multiple internal levels. Pursuing imagined destinies literally connects a single strand of our energy in one potential future, while another filament is sent forward to an alternate vision. Ultimately, these may or—more importantly—may not come to pass. When those future potentials do not manifest in the way our imagination designed, what happens with all those energies we dispersed? This is why we often feel we are running to catch up with ourselves. We are trying to reclaim all the life energy we have carelessly misplaced, while still chasing in new mental imageries.

Destiny is the *now* of destination. Release the pursuit. Become the continuum of destiny fulfilling itself, in each new and wondrous instant. Remember, our destiny is a given. We choose it every morning when we wake, and with every step we take. With each of these days and steps, choices are made, actions are taken and destiny is created. Despite our attempts to greatly complicate the experience, life is truly this simple. Our internal scuffles have never been—and will never be—a contributor to the fulfillment of destiny. Relax, and let your destiny lead you into the potential surprises awaiting you. Release attachment to all the energy of those imagined futures. Then trust that life is a continuing adventure of discovery just because you have chosen that it be so. Be fully present in all the minutes of your day and you allow the destiny you have already chosen to unfold. There is no ritual or process for this except being present, and enjoying the delight of arriving at the unforeseeable junctures of life.

Allowing your inner wisdom to chart its own course in meeting its own destiny by letting that destiny fulfill itself is an amazing act of friendship, combined with unfettered loyalty to yourself. The only help our inner wisdom has ever needed was for our minds to release the reins and let it flow. Befriend all the human and energetic levels of yourself. Release the destiny of your being. Sit back, and enjoy the wonder of witnessing it explode into its own fullness.

We have led ourselves on this walk of chasing, defining, sculpting, and shaping ourselves to create the opportunity to say "Now, because the work was done, we are okay; because the work was completed, we are perfection; because the work to become so was undertaken, we are worthy." But what has been true from the beginning, and remains so unto *now*, is that we have always been okay, always been worthy. We have always been perfect. There is no, was no, work to do. Now as we also acknowledge the vital contribution made by our human levels, we become even more of the more that we are as expressed in this physical realm.

This idea called "work" has been a primary limitation to all on the path of understanding their innate insight and perfection. The presumptions and labor that were born of the idea have served as the thrust for pushing ourselves, demanding of ourselves, judging ourselves for not accomplishing, and projecting upon ourselves an idea of a reduced level of deservingness.

Rather than work, we are here to *be life*, to live blissfully and lovingly through physical experience. We are invited to live this amazing reality of physicality for the pure sake of being able to do so. We are not here as worker bees, subject to the approval or withholding of some unseen force. Our inner wisdom does not require—does not even desire—that we prove ourselves through any action of work or labor. We are here to play in a wondrous new expression of self-realization. We are here to experience emotions through a human body. We are here to be physically enlivened by the amazing sensations of taste, touch, sight, scent, and hearing. We are here to play in this world and to play inclusively and transparently with each other. We are here to share our individual gifts as an offering for collective upliftment.

The gifts we desire to share with one another are not within us as a directive toward a path of work. Think of the word gift, what it means and implies. Our gifts are treasures which when shared, enhance both our own life and the lives of our brothers and sisters. Playing in our gifts stimulates their energy, which frees our passion. Within this lives the thrill of experiencing their animated fulfillment. This is how, when freely expressed, they "gift" equally to the giver and the receiver. The visceral pleasure found within this perceptual transformation is witnessed as our gifts present their greatest potential to bless, enliven, and inspire anyone they touch. In generous return, the gift teaches us how to *be life*.

Having released all effort, as we take up our gifts with focus we begin riding the waves of our passion and allowing it to flame audaciously through the sharing of our natural talents.

Additionally freeing to our passion is setting aside the time-worn motivation to persist in work as a support-mechanism to our belief that; if we prevail and stick to the path we will earn great rewards. Waiting for a reward is looking outside our self for a level of validation we are not willing to bestow upon ourselves.

Now as we shift from beneath the limiting idea of work, the gifts with which we are endowed are emerging—as this very reward. Simple recognition of the potential unification our gifts carry and the liberty they have the ability to afford us, are rewards beyond any vision we have ever dared to anticipate.

Our very existence as Human Beingness endowed with freedom of choice and action is a definitive reward. Through this, anything we desire—and more than we can imagine—is ours in a single, brilliant flash, as soon as we say "yes" and relax. One simple "yes" and we are positioned to experience a greater level of validation than we could ever have thought to request; an endless well of self-love for our mere presence, without qualification.

Continuing to look for any reward will negate this. It activates the old belief that we lack an authentic infusion of life presence, that we still believe we are less than passion-guided humanness. It reveals a lingering perception that this universe metes out its blessings based on personal performance or a compliant adherence to specific rules and requirements. Accepting that it *might just be possible* that we are each recipients of all the blessings, of all that is, in every moment, initiates the unraveling of these limiting convictions. Even— sincerely—acknowledging the possibility undermines the need for specific or randomly offered reward.

What a wonderful respite ceasing to chase rewards is presenting. Center in the amazing being you are. As you expand your comfort with *being life*, miraculous surprises will continue to manifest in an endless waterfall of blessings sure to vastly enrich your existence with an unending renewal of self-trust.

As an exhibition of distrust, many times we have heard someone speak of their "work" and the desire to move forward with it, followed with the list of reasons why they have not been able to fulfill their mission. This has typically been accompanied by an expression of angst over when spirit, the universe, their higher selves, the Gods of karma, will bestow upon them the long-withheld elements.

We are each far too wise to enter physical life and undertake a path of destiny without the accompaniment of our own inner wisdom fueled by an inextinguishable passion, to complete that walk. Each of us entered this physical life with an assured knowingness that within its days we would see through the illusions created by our commitment to the prevailing societal structures. In their absence re-embracing genuine self-awareness by actualizing self-trust becomes an emerging organic flow.

Pending that eye-opening revelation we demonstrate our absence of self-trust in exceedingly creative ways. Each new approach is designed to offer further illustration of the reasons trusting ourselves is a foolhardy consideration. Subsequently, we have tempted and teased ourselves; we have led ourselves down every potholed path we could find. And when we could not find one severe enough, we would locate a shovel, dig deeper holes, and then toss ourselves in.

Through all of this, we have continued to progress in our remembrance of who we are and have always been. Even when we tethered ourselves to every post we came upon and tied our energy secure with the strongest rope we could create, we have pulled free of them all.

This is why so much of our life experience has focused on the re-development of absolute trust. Now we are seeing that all we need do is stop instigating *distrust* of ourselves. This is not to say that we must release every fear that might ever rise in any situation. The truth is, this is precisely what we have been attempting to do through our on-going struggles. Many of our anxieties are rooted in our attempt to derail any *potential* fear before it has time to fully form.

The silliness of attempting to dissolve fears not yet established requires imagining what they might be, what might ignite them, how they might feel, and in which ways they might restrict us. In short, we have manufactured fear to avoid being caught unaware by it at some later time. And still we have been surprised.

Retire this nonsensical habit and the internal tug-o-wars that ensue from it will fall away. Practice simply trusting yourself. Trust that whatever fears do arise, you are equipped to address them through the studies you have already pursued and the additional wisdom you will gain in living from this time to the occurrence of their emergence. Through this, trust will be will reactivated in each of the ways in which you have always been deserving.

Through every quest to re-embody trust, what we have feared most deeply is trusting ourselves with the generously given gift of Free Will Choice and the exhalation that playing in it evokes. If this were not true, we would have long ago opened our lives to its ever-present availability. Instead we feared becoming lost in the freedom, confused by it. We feared becoming lost in the enjoyment, overwhelmed by its abundant stimulation. Further, we have feared making a choice that could result in a second crushing loss of these reclaimed treasures after having finally re-embraced them. But then they were never lost, only silenced and suppressed.

As we open our eyes and remember how to listen to life with all of our senses, we begin to *notice* that we were never actually cut off from any gift given or authentic self-expression. Our gift of choice and the use of it will remain, always, a part of our reality. It is an essential aspect of the whole of who we are, not an externalized element that can be carried away. Any loss of our innate wisdom or happiness is little more than evidence of our commitment to the idea of loss. No natural element or expression of our wholeness has ever been withdrawn, only disowned.

It is as true now, as has ever been, that we have the option to instantly shift into our naturally boundless and passion-filled state. One of the most effective tools we have implemented in distancing ourselves from the vastness that we are is Free Will Choice. We have applied it by opting to avoid remembering that being lost in our organic flow of ecstatic passion, lost in the comfort of our internal wisdom, was the greatest exhilaration we have ever known, the most sincere authenticity we have ever expressed.

Now we are collectively emancipating ourselves by ceasing to work, strive, struggle, compete and compare, in any way. Abandoning the addiction to effort is one of the most uplifting gifts we have ever offered to our own beings as it is giving us space and oxygen to resume a natural state of being. Every idea of work is based in self-judgments that insist wholeness can and must be earned. As we now know, the Law of Physics dictates that we can have anything we desire—a home, new employment, health—by doing nothing more than matching our energetic pulse to that frequency. That being so, how can this be any less true of self-trust, internal peace, joyfulness of mind, emotion, and sensory experience? Living authentically inspires the humane treatment of yourself that spontaneously dissolves every one of these judgments.

Within each burden we have placed upon ourselves and every limitation we have imagined, one constant has eluded our awareness. Only authentic Beingness could prevail within such powerful odds as what we have self-perpetuated. This self-inflicted pressure to single-handedly navigate our way into the channel of personal wholeness speaks volumes to the truth that; in disassociating from trust we also surrendered our ability to love fully.

So now can you love yourself? Will you choose to love yourself? That is the only question that is left for any of us. Ultimately, there can be only one answer. Love and trust are two faces of the same expression. We are both Divine Beings and Human Beings, bonded into a single, united experience of life. Therefore, at our core we are nothing but love, so yes, we can love ourselves. If the operative is "can," we are incapable of less. Moreover if the operative is "can," we are also incapable of not loving *every single* level, expression and presentation of ourselves.

But will you? Will you choose to activate the love that you are—here, now, in this moment, and for all the many days to come? The only other option is to continue to pretend to be something else, something other, something less than that which is true and real.

Practice being a courageous and valiant friend to yourself. In doing so, you will become a friend to your mind that has served so tirelessly, and it will be released from the burdens under which it has labored. Moving beyond the intrigues of the mind and resting peacefully in your heart is a heroic shift to befriending yourself. As your mind relaxes and realizes it has progressed beyond the illusions of separation, you become equipped to be a friend to your gifts— formerly called work—inviting them to express themselves through your experience of *being life*.

Being a friend to yourself is a most generous means of establishing an intimate relationship with every level of your mental, emotional and sensory self. Through this friendship, your inner wisdom is given permission to run free. As you no longer restrict it to carefully selected places throughout your body and throughout life, it can enhance all of your moments in each of the ways it has longed to.

And it is most certainly time to be a friend to your innate Beingness. Allow it to be unburdened of the oppression of your mind's over-activity, and to become fully embraced as the radiance of wholeness—the presence of authentic Beingness. Healing is not based in what we *do to* the levels of our being, but in how much we are willing to love ourselves, our whole selves, just as we are. Being a friend to ourselves is as easy as getting out of our own way, offering ourselves the space and oxygen to care for our own beings in all the many ways we know, and to play in the discovery of new and expanded expressions of loving self-care. Loving ourselves is also expressed by loving the life that infuses us by munificently sharing a love of life with all we encounter.

Through this is born a new willingness and readiness to realize all that we are. We become ready to recognize ourselves as the love of which we were created. This positions us to feel the extensive reach of our creative powers. And finally, we express the absolute limitlessness of our every capacity, our fullest aliveness.

It is no secret that we fear our power. But why is that? This hesitancy supports the primal fear that tells us that if we reach the top of the mountain, there is nowhere to go but back down. It is an ironic paradox we have created; chasing a perfected destination while fearing into great avoidance that very achievement. The dreaded potential of having to retrace that path—downward—sends tremors of panic through all of our levels of consciousness—primal, emotional, and cellular. The fear speaks to us through quakes of indefinable anxiety and registers as a deterrent to following any path that might truly surprise us.

If we first speak honestly to ourselves, acknowledge that this mountain has no top, and that we have always possessed inner wisdom and vibrancy, then we will simply continue into further and broader expansion. This will allow us to put the entire body of worry to rest.

We have revisited the numerous injuries of our past over and again to remind ourselves to do nothing that could result in a replay of our endless mistakes. From our primal memory, that is how we view our life in the physical realm—as a body of grave errors that continually leave us retracing old paths and withdrawing steps once thought to be complete.

But when looking boldly into life, we remember what the greatest lesson really is. Life continues. Regardless of what we choose, life continues.

Breathe into your inner wisdom. It understands that each new horizon is another in a series of plateaus all positioned for a long ascent that has no actual completion. Stay, play, enjoy, any plateau for as long as you please. And when you feel ready to move on, your inner wisdom also knows where every ladder to the next is placed. You see, this life was never meant to be a continual struggle up a great and rocky hill, only a series of continually elevating vistas from which to enjoy the tremendous expanse of all that is. And lest it be forgotten, this has never been and will never be a realm of conclusion. There is no ending possible by embracing ourselves wholly. All imagined threat is lifted from us by acknowledging our human life as an experience of tremendous value and surprising potentialities.

The unavoidable emancipation within these acknowledgements brings a close to this strenuous and challenging section of life's journey. From here forward, it is no longer necessary to tread the tedious path of climbing and scraping and skinning our elbows while periodically sliding backwards a bit. The illusions that drove those mis-adventures have collapsed, like balloons whose air has escaped.

Be as you are. Play freely. Experience and express Free Will Choice. Live your joyousness. Feel your passion of life burning and invigorating. Move gracefully into the experience of life by hearing, feeling, and expressing the voices of your emotions and senses, now in harmonious balance with each other.

This is our time. Do not hold back; do not recoil. Just take the leap. Then rest in the newly resurrected knowledge that all that is good, wise, gentle, and loving is already manifesting through, to, and around you in all of the most glorious and abundant ways ever witnessed by you at any time, in any place. This is your mirror, the most honest mirror you have ever allowed. Dive in and enjoy.

Part III

Coming Home

Just Roll Over and Float

How we have been struggling. Struggling with life, struggling with our personalities, struggling with our asserted identities, struggling with our projected judgments, struggling in rejection of physical life as being an exile from some indefinable 'better' place, struggling to hang onto our physical existence for fear of ceasing to be, struggling with each other to avoid witnessing the mirrors we offer to one another, and struggling with our stories. The recitation is dizzying and living the struggle has been nothing short of chronically exhausting. It is time to embrace the fullness of our whole selves, our Divinity and our Humanity in unified harmony. Further, it is time we allow our innate completeness to replace the action of pretending to be all lesser mental expressions.

There have been occasions during each of our lives when we tapped into free flowing joy. Maybe for a moment, perhaps for a day, we have each known it, felt it, lived it on various occasions—albeit too few. The reason we were able to do this at all is because within us—in every second of our lives—exists a core of that pure joy.

Recall an experience of deep laughter. Close your eyes and connect with the instant you felt it moving through you. It is a body of energy that rolls up from deeply within, is it not? Our joy is not a blanket that comes from outside to cover and surround, but a natural movement of what is already an integral part of us.

We seek happiness as a precious butterfly—always floating on the air—just beyond our fingertips. At our core, we are Divine Presence.

Could it possibly be true that this awareness—our soul—is anything but ecstatic at the opportunity to share in the breadth of experience available only through this magnificent physical world?

All we are is but a breath away, resting peacefully within our heart, our senses, our cells. As soon as we begin moving forward in life, as if this is true, we will experience the reality of it. Enter each day focused on allowing all that is astonishing and wise within to lead you gently from one minute, one encounter to the next.

To know peace within ourselves, within life, to allow our joy to be a daily expression, it is time to *Just Roll Over and Float*. This is traditionally a river kayaking term. It means that when your kayak tips over—and they all do at some time—just float in the natural arc of the river. It will eventually carry you out of the rushing waters at the center to the safety of the shoreline. On the other hand, if you try to swim, or grab onto something, you are likely to bring injury or worse upon yourself.

In the context of our daily life, to *Just Roll Over and Float* is to live the grace of our entire Divinity as expressed through our ever-exuberant Humanity. To *Roll Over and Float* is to become fluid within yourself and your life. It is the action of living your joy, rather than the mind's constructs. As this becomes the norm, you cease to think in terms of all the things you are going to do when, as soon as, after this or that. You remember the only thing stopping you is the belief in a need to wait.

This new approach to life cannot be understood by studying or engaging in the wanderings of our mind. To *Just Roll Over and Float* means no longer pushing for an answer, or a specific definition. Breathe the query into your body, and go about your day. Have some fun. Instead of one directive-based answer, what will rise to the surface of your consciousness is a full realization of your most gentle option(s). Through this, you will access all the levels of your innate inner wisdom. And it occurs far more expeditiously if you are moving, laughing, experiencing life than when you were sitting wandering through your mind in ad nauseam pursuit.

In addition to what we have asked of our minds, up to this point we have also been largely focused on the outer world to tell us what to do, think and feel. An essential expression of *Rolling Over and Floating* is being in the *now*, which is easily achieved by practicing the many ways you can enjoy your physical self and the world at large. It is our human self that centers us directly into the *now*, for that is the space from which our life emanates.

Release dependency on the outer world to offer you the answers, only carried within. The external world was never meant to be a director to our lives, but a mirror, reflecting that which we carry within the internal levels of our beings. It is the return to this inner voice—the voice that speaks to us through our human cells—that refocuses our attention in the direction of our most easily accessible truth.

In becoming accustomed to the life practice of *Just Roll Over and Float*, remember that letting go is not the same as giving up. As one gives up, they relinquish all acknowledgment that they do have power and choice in their lives. Letting go is the act of releasing control, surrendering the need to know every detail of what is moving through your life in advance of its arrival, and why it is presenting itself at this specific time. The habit has been to do this while maintaining the position of suspicion and non-acceptance until the mental review is complete, and the opportunity has been approved or dismissed.

Letting go initiates understanding throughout your being that you have inherent access to a great wealth of wisdom and guidance within. It is the acknowledgement that you are the living embodiment of wisdom, and that you maintain access to that through your days.

Letting go is the recognition that your deepest inner self desires—above all things—to enjoy a fulfilled life and that you possess the human intelligence to be led in that very direction.

Letting go carries you beyond the restrictions of your mind, and its constructs, into the action of *Just Rolling Over and Floating* within your days while experiencing complete satisfaction.

As one does release their mind to its own well-deserved peace and adopts a *Just Roll Over and Float* approach to life, they often experience a false sensation of identity loss. This is not a loss of identity at all, but a release of definition created by the personality and asserted identities. Freeing ourselves of these rigid boundaries liberates us from the limitations into which they had held us restricted. Releasing these masks created of the fear of our self brings us to empowered personhood. We begin to live as a true Human Being, a full expression of the greater All that we are, in open receptivity to the flow of everything that life offers.

The most important realization around *Just Rolling Over and Floating* is that it can only be achieved through playing with the experience. All actions of trying are contrary to the entire adventure. Further, it is not a meditation, a mantra, or temporary practice. To *Just Roll Over and Float* is the act of living fully, every day of your life. Release the fight for survival that is common to all of humankind by ceasing to engage in all struggle, control, and competition. Set aside the habit of battering your mind, body, senses, and emotions, by beginning to address yourself in the most lovingly supportive ways. To *Just Roll Over and Float* is to care for ourselves, all levels of ourselves, in a completely humane manner—in all moments. To *Just Roll Over and Float* is acting toward our self, and all others, as the embodiment of wisdom, love, and playfulness manifest.

Living Life

An ever-increasing percentage of people on the planet are practicing a constant drive to find wholeness. Wholeness cannot be found like a trinket that has rolled under a chair. It can only be experienced, and this can only occur by living it.

A whole and authentic life is not spent buried in books, not spent in prayer circles or meditation rituals, not spent in therapy rooms or an endless succession of self-improvement events, not spent being afraid to turn the stereo above three or bond with those of completely differing beliefs and interests. It may include some of these activities, but not from the flight inducing perspectives of fear. Any sensation of being afraid, leads us away from an actualized life, and holds us captive to the search for context. So each of these activities only benefit us to the extent that they are choices to move toward the self, existing as additional components to a life full with other exchanges and expressions.

Although frequently spoken of in minimizing language our human body and senses are as important an aspect to living a complete life, as is our inner wisdom. A life lived wholly is spent eating amazing food and enjoying every calorie, having great sex with a beloved, and dancing with your whole body, mind, and spirit until you can barely move the next day, then waking to languor within your sheets smiling at the exuberance of the experience. This is the embodiment of an authentic life.

To truly and fully live, one must *feel* life, *taste* life, *be* life. The renowned writer Emile' Zola once stated:

*"If you ask me what I came into this life to do, I will tell you:
I came to live out loud."*

Be actualized wisdom expressing humanness. Live boldly, live loudly, live with full commitment to being in the body of life, not sitting on the sidelines with a book, notepad, and pen, quietly making observations and taking notes.

It is time to come out of the cloistered confines of a self-created classroom and dive into the most magnificent field of learning that will ever be available to us—life. As you rise from your study and struggle to begin with a totally new set of experiences of living wholly, you begin to understand the vastness of a life only available through full sensory participation.

We each have models in and around our lives, friends, and associations who do live in a full way, who have grasped the understanding that living is the action of being *consciously* alive. The people we each find closest to us are those with whom we share the most in common. How many of those dearest to you also model full sensory living? How many within your intimate circle live with such uninhibited passion as to inspire not only their closest friends and family, but all with whom they come in contact? What traits and traditions are those most closely bonded to you emulating? What are the points of similarity between them as a group, between them and you?

Are they committed to living the fullest experience offered in each moment of every day? Do they exude the radiance of happy people with full lives and richly intimate relationships?

Are they involved in life beyond the parameters of their immediate family, work, and close personal friends? Do they reach out to the world at large through community service, volunteerism, political activism, social advocacy, and then come back to share of the enrichment this offered?

Is traveling—enjoying new and unfamiliar environments, gaining wisdom from varying cultures, drinking in the many different sights and sounds that this world has to share, to educate through, and to simply enjoy—a regular part of their life?

Can you sit and chat with them about the great novels you have each read, or the new musician you only just discovered, the amazing film you recently attended?

How varied are your associations? What is the breadth of your daily experience? This is the mirror reflection of your own level of comfort in engaging with the wide range of possibilities available to each of us in this world.

Passion—The Fire of Life

As we reflect on those who do live fully and boldly, the one thing that can be observed in each of them is a brightly burning passion for life itself. Passion is often spoken of in context with one's degree of engagement with life. From many directions, we are told to live our passion, follow our passion, but then we are also told—directly and passively—that we must only do this quietly, sedately.

This is not passion. It is not a silent flame that burns unnoticed. To experience passion is to become passion. Living our passion, becoming its essence is flowing into the completely unrestrained, uncalculated space of expressing the fire that is always burning in the center of our beings. This is the fire of life, the invigorating pulse that reaches out beyond itself—inspiring and enriching the lives of all it touches. To live passion is to feel that fire for any moment or execution of life. Embracing this sacred element of who we each are requires that we move beyond our own boundaries, beyond all desire to hide any level of ourselves from ourselves, or anyone else.

We each came to this life with a passion for our own beings, and a passionate desire to know more of ourselves through this realm of physical presentation. We carried within us a passion for the others with whom we were embarking on this adventure, and a passion for the adventure itself. As to the Humane expressions that we would become, we carried an unbridled passion for all that they would allow us to see, know, and experience.

We understood that passion is the self-sustaining energy that grows on and within itself, feeding every exchange and opportunity to enhance our existence. And just as we understood the infinite nature of our own wisdom, we also knew that the fire of life called passion can never die.

Passion is literally the fire that burns inside for the purpose of giving life to each of us. It rises to speak when we think or feel around that which is most dear to our inner selves, and all that we are most committed to expressing in this life. It compels us toward the paths sure to be most enriching to our human levels of self. As it burns, and we move in the direction of its leading, the fire expands. Unlike physical fires that absorb oxygen, this fire is the exact thing that feeds us beyond anything else available. The higher it burns, the greater the amount of energy it draws to and through each level of our beingness. It carries us forward in ways of compassionate action that instill each of us with a deep knowing of our value in the world, and therein, the absolute significance of all.

It is passion that leads us to our most fulfilling experiences, that supports us in living the boldest and most enriched life available. As this occurs, we are constantly stepping beyond the borders of our personal comfort zones, thereby, expanding the comfort zone itself.

Through this, others are magnetized by our expanding frequency to play freely, and we become the teachers to each other of our ever-existent flow with the miraculous nature of this world, by realizing that we are physically manifested miracles.

Being in the physical world and also in possession of the ability to co-create our lives is a miracle. Our innate Humane Presence is a miracle in the way it supports us and all that is life. Our mind, so often committed to its own inner torment has also found a way to lead us to this point of self-realization, self-actualization. This is absolutely a miraculous occurrence. We are—on all levels and in all ways—miracles of existence.

Gandhi once said:
Be the change you want to see in the world.

How about:
Be the miracle you wish to experience in your life.

Everything that would be required to accomplish this is already within. Live that truth. Live that wholeness. Be the miracle that you are.

Just Say Yes

The clearest, most uncomplicated path to being the externally expressed passion of your internal fire, being the miracle that is the whole of you, is found in *Just Saying Yes*.

Yes is the power of life in movement, the current of the river we *Roll Over and Float* within as we are carried to safety. In every second of life, there is a *yes* present somewhere. Life, when lived authentically, is the stance of opening one's arms to the universe within and the world without, and just saying *yes*.

Yes is not simply a word. It is a path of living. As we learn to follow that path, or rest within that current, it will weave us through all of the winding trails of life, blessing our journey with the most amazing experience, while showing us solutions to each challenge that presents itself. The path of *yes* is found by being most gentle toward and honoring of the self, while embracing every new opportunity to move in any shifting direction.

But how can this be when life appears so full of invitations to say *no?* You join a friend for dinner. They pick you up and drive you to the selected restaurant. At the end of the evening, they are a bit intoxicated. How do you say *yes*, and still honor yourself, your safety? Say *yes* to choosing an alternate means of transportation home. Honor yourself while allowing your energy to remain open and free flowing.

Each time you travel the path of *no*, you close your energy down—not only to what you are saying *no* to, but to anything else that would want to be presented in your direction. You cannot close the door to keep the mosquitoes out while still leaving it open for the cat to come in. It is really that simple. We say *no* to any one potential, and we close our energy to many others that we cannot imagine—and now, will not have the chance to entertain. When we say no, our mind and energy hears *no*. It does not delineate what direction we are closing off, only that we do not want to receive in that moment.

Saying *yes* is the ultimate act of self-trust in the river of life. As we say *yes* to life, without first scrutinizing what we are saying *yes* to, we invite life to shower us in ways that our finite minds cannot conceive. In this, we have not relinquished our Free Will Choice. Rather, we have offered ourselves a vastly expanded array of amusements from which to choose. Each *yes* leaves your internal channels open to more life flow, which leads you to another set of choices. Feel—not think—but *feel*, deeply into each situation, find the *yes* and follow the natural current. Release the old tradition of yes/no, right/wrong. *Just Say Yes* and let life share with you the thrill of being wholly, fully alive.

Is It Fun Being You

How many times recently have you flung your arms around yourself with the exclamation, "I love being me!" or "I love my life!"? Was it a true exclamation, free of restriction and inhibition?

Does performing the tasks or service you engage in through your work cause you to—spontaneously—sit back in complete satisfaction that this is how you get to spend your time? And in addition to that, you actually create income in the process!

What are the elements of your life that stimulate these responses of joy at being who you are? How much time are you willing to spend experiencing this level of fulfillment?

Say *yes* to expanding that time. *Just Roll Over and Float* and allow your inner wisdom to guide you into creation of these larger spaces of enjoyment. Say *yes* to having fun being you. Allow the path of *yes* to illuminate the adventures you have chosen to create with that one all-powerful choice expressed through a single word.

Who in your life inspires the greatest joy when you are together? How much time do you offer yourself to spend with this person? Are you willing to expand this as well? The more we surround ourselves with those who have already begun to flow this freely, the more we learn about how we too can make choices that enrich, fulfill, and entertain us to the deepest potential.

What do you want to do that you never "find time" to pursue? When are you going to give yourself the opportunity to find out if this is something that fulfills you, or does it feel safer to hold it at a distance? Is *not* achieving this dream the motivation that sustains you from one day, year, and decade to the next? You are a creator. There is no need to fear running out of creations with which to play. If what you do create proves to be less than you desired, you are still a creator. Congratulate yourself for receiving what you had chosen, have fun with the moment of self-acknowledgement. Then proceed to make new and varied choices. A great deal of the fun in life is discovered in the creating itself, and the openness of allowing yourself to be excited about the ability *to* create, endlessly.

Is it fun being you? If not, what are you willing to trust yourself to embrace that will enrich your life? Much time and focus has been placed on releasing what is not comfortable. In other words, a preponderance of time is spent dwelling in *noticing* your discomfort. The more gentle way to accomplish release is to show yourself that life *can be* fun—even for you—by embracing the expansiveness and nature of each new day, and remembering that you have the power to choose a new direction in any instant. As you consciously allow more and broader contentment, the dreary corners you have long struggled against are released because there is simply less room left for them to reside in your awareness.

It is time to lead a fully invigorated life, which is primarily expressed through our human self, our senses, emotions, and our passion-filled actions. Involve yourself deeply in the textures and sensations of the life that you are living. Retire from the struggle, and play in your life. Play within your work, play within your gifts, play within your body, mind, and opportunities.

Will you let down all the screens, protections and guard towers that filter out too much of what life is offering you? Are you willing to trust that you cannot know the answers because you have not yet heard the questions? Can you feel how you are always protected, you are eternally supported? Can you let life and its challenges flow unrestricted and trust that you are prepared for each new opportunity?

Are you willing to *Just Say Yes* to the question: Is it fun being you? Will you relax and *Just Roll Over and Float,* allow your inner guidance, your life itself, to carry you into overflowing satisfaction through all that it offers?

Life was meant to be a grand adventure. We came here for the simple joy of being here. Set down your books. Retire all your mental stresses. Don't worry, if you miss the unrest and worries too much your mind can make up new ones for you. But take a chance. Begin this moment to redesign the way in which you design your life, for it is yours and you are the creator, so have some fun being you.

Life as an Artform

You are the artist *of* your life in that you possess the power of creation through your engagement with Free Will Choice. How are you going to illustrate the moments and hours of your days? Will they be full of texture, vibrant in their very existence? Will they be full of sounds and music of every type? How will you use the shadows to best enhance the rays of light? For they can do this very thing, if you so choose.

Be comfortably, intimately, familiar with yourself, and in that, available to extend intimately to the others with whom you share this life.

This is your journey. It is completely up to you what flavors, scents, and sensations it will be filled with. It is you who will choose the ways in which the mirrors will bounce light into every single cell of your being, of your life.

We are the leaders of our times, the elders to all those who come after us, and will continue to come. We cannot be leaders if we are still wandering around like little lost lambs, struggling, and reaching for wholeness while whining about our absence of peace. Stop searching for the peaceful oneness that has always rested within you.

It is time for each of us to rise to the responsibility we already have the internal power to fulfill. We are ready to live the humane expressions that are our innate inner truth. Through this, life will inspire each of us to amazing heights, and our newly discovered exhilaration will spread to all those we each touch, inviting every person we encounter to live life to its fullest.

Life *is* the power with the ability to reach into our depths. Life itself will raise us up to save ourselves, each other, and ultimately, all life on this glorious planet that has been so generously gifted to us as an amazing playground of adventure.

Acknowledgements

It took a community to bring this book to life. The journey of completion was challenging, revealing and would not have been possible without the encouragement, participation, enthusiasm, collaboration and support of many people.

I offer abounding appreciation to Sharon Rose, Rosalie Grace, Wendy Walsh, Jerielle Young, Carol Ann Jerome, McCarty Baker, Scott Johnson, Bonnie Thompson, Karen Kuhl, Jaye Newman, Lei'ohu Ryder and Maydeen Iao.

As *Just Roll Over and Float* is the result of a series of curriculums that spanned several years, I am immensely grateful to all the participants who ultimately became some of my most precious teachers.

This being a primarily self-edited work, I invite you to enjoy the context and forgive the grammatical mis-steps.

CPSIA information can be obtained at www.ICGtesting.com
Printed in the USA
LVOW060627291211

261535LV00001B/6/P